God
in All Moments

Mystical & Practical Spiritual Wisdom from Hasidic Masters

Edited and Translated by **Or N. Rose**

with Ebn D. Leader

For People of All Faiths, All Backgrounds

JEWISH LIGHTS Publishing

Woodstock, Vermont

God in All Moments:
Mystical & Practical Spiritual Wisdom from Hasidic Masters

2004 First Printing
© 2004 by Or N. Rose with Ebn D. Leader

Library of Congress Cataloging-in-Publication Data

God in all moments : mystical & practical spiritual wisdom from Hasidic masters / translated and edited Or N. Rose with Ebn D. Leader.
        p. cm.
ISBN 1-58023-186-1
    1. Hasidism—Quotations, maxims, etc. 2. Spiritual life—Judaism.
3.Hasidim—Customs and practices. I. Rose, Or N. II. Leader, Ebn D.,
1969–
    BM198.2.G64 2003
    296´7—dc22   2003019394

10 9 8 7 6 5 4 3 2 1

Manufactured in the United States of America

Published by Jewish Lights Publishing
A Division of LongHill Partners, Inc.
Sunset Farm Offices, Route 4, P.O. Box 237
Woodstock, VT 05091
Tel: (802) 457-4000   Fax: (802) 457-4004
www.jewishlights.com

We dedicate this book to our beloved teacher,

Rabbi Arthur Green

"Find yourself a teacher; acquire a friend."

(*Pirke Avot* 1:6)

Contents

Introduction

Hasidism, the great mystical revival movement, swept through Eastern Europe in the late eighteenth century, capturing the hearts and minds of nearly half the Jewish population in a matter of decades.[1] The spiritual founder of this movement was Israel ben Eliezer, the Ba'al Shem Tov (the "Master of the Good Name," 1700–1760). A charismatic folk healer,[2] the Ba'al Shem Tov stood at the center of a small group of mystics who together developed a new religious vision for Judaism.[3] The Besht (the acronym by which he is often called) preached a message of hope and inspiration, calling on Jews of different social and educational backgrounds to awaken to God's immanent presence in the world. Gleaning insights from a wide variety of previous kabbalistic[4] materials, the early Hasidim stressed the importance of mystical contemplation, joyful religious service, and intentional living.

While the Ba'al Shem Tov was Hasidism's first great personality, it was his disciple, Rabbi Dov Baer, the Maggid ("Preacher") of Mezeritch (d. 1772),[5] who was responsible for the creation of the movement. The "Great Maggid" was both a gifted teacher and a skillful organizer. He gathered around himself an impressive group of young scholars, creating one of the outstanding spiritual brotherhoods in Jewish history. The members of this group included Levi Isaac of Berditchev, Shneor Zalman of Liadi (founder of HaBaD, or Lubavitch Hasidism), Menahem Nahum of Chernobyl, and the brothers Elimelech of Lizensk and Zusia of Anipol.[6] Under the tutelage of the

Great Maggid, these men developed into creative thinkers, inspiring preachers, and persuasive missionaries. The members of the Maggid's circle set forth from their master's study house poised to convert Eastern European Jewry to the ways of Hasidism. Despite meeting immediate and intense opposition from members of the existing rabbinic and social establishment (known as the Mitnaggedim, "Opponents"),[7] these pioneering figures soon transformed the Jewish landscape of Eastern Europe, leaving an indelible mark on Judaism up to the present day.[8]

In the past several decades, many people beyond the traditional Hasidic world have turned to the teachings of the Hasidic masters for inspiration and guidance. This is, of course, part of a larger cultural phenomenon in which increasing numbers of spiritual seekers have looked to the classical religious traditions of the world—particularly the mystical strands within these traditions—in search of meaning.[9] In the case of Hasidism, the two forms of teaching that have received the greatest attention from modern spiritual seekers are the *derashot* (homilies, sermons) and the *sippurim* (tales told by the Hasidic masters and legends about the masters as told by their followers). It was the renowned German Jewish thinker Martin Buber (1878–1965) who first brought the tales to the West at the beginning of the twentieth century, offering a creative (and idiosyncratic) reading of this material that stressed the humanistic character of these writings.[10] Gershom Scholem (1897–1982), Buber's compatriot and archcritic, pioneered the study of the sermons. As the creator of the academic study of Jewish mysticism, Scholem carefully dissected these works, attempting to understand the doctrinal underpinnings—theological and ideological—of the

Hasidic masters.[11] Since the days of these two intellectual giants, many other scholars and religious interpreters have added to our understanding of the history and thought of Hasidism.[12]

However, one area of Hasidic lore that has not yet received much attention from seekers or scholars is a genre of literature known as *hanhagot*, "spiritual practices."[13] Appended to many collections of Hasidic homilies (or contained within various anthologies) are short lists of instructions created by the Hasidic masters for their followers. These brief teachings are designed to aid the devotee in applying the Hasidic ideals to daily life. Often, the Rebbes ("Rabbis," Hasidic masters in Yiddish) would advise their disciples to copy these instructions and carry them in their pockets throughout the day, reading them whenever they required spiritual guidance or centering. The *hanhagot* have a practical tone that is mostly absent from the more theoretical homilies or the mythical tales. They include guidance for prayer, advice on personal and interpersonal affairs, and tools (such as mantras and visualization exercises) for maintaining one's mystical focus while at work or when traveling.

The Hasidic Rebbes, however, were not the originators of this literary form. Rather, it was the sixteenth-century mystics of Safed (in northern Israel) who first developed the practice of writing *hanhagot*. Several individuals from the circles of Moses Cordovero and Isaac Luria[14] created lists of spiritual directives for themselves and their disciples. The Safed *hanhagot* have both a mystical and an ascetic character. The devotee is strongly encouraged to undertake a strict regimen of self-mortification, including fasting, sleep deprivation, and the avoidance of bathing and perfuming, as preparation for mystical experience.[15]

The practice of writing *hanhagot* continued in various Jewish mystical circles from the sixteenth century onward. While the Hasidic directives are similar in many respects to earlier *hanhagot,* they also have a specifically Hasidic character. This includes a restriction on ascetic practices and a new focus on joy as a spiritual imperative. The Hasidic Rebbes also placed special emphasis on the possibility of encountering the Divine in all areas of life— in the marketplace, while traveling or conversing with friends, and even during sexual relations. Like the Hasidic movement as a whole, the *hanhagot* represent a careful selection and reworking of earlier religious values and traditions.

By making these texts available in English, we hope to share this inspiring form of Hasidic wisdom with a broad range of spiritual seekers, both Jewish and non-Jewish. The *hanhagot* offer us insightful and practical suggestions for contemplative living, and their direct and relatively straightforward style invites both the initiated and the beginner into an authentic dialogue with the Jewish mystical tradition. While the *hanhagot* are often formulated as prescriptive lessons—handed down from master to disciple with definite "do's" and "don'ts"—we encourage you to glean freely from this material, incorporating those teachings that are most helpful to you at a particular moment or stage of life. To this end, we have often placed texts with different (even contradictory) messages side by side within each section of the book.

In editing this volume, we have selected those texts that we believe are both representative of the genre as a whole and resonant with contemporary spiritual sensibilities. Therefore, we have consciously omitted materials that are egregiously sexist, racist, or offensive in other respects.[16]

The texts included in this volume come from several early Hasidic sources, mostly from the circles of the Besht and the Great Maggid. Some were originally designed for mass distribution and others intended for a smaller group of learned mystics.[17] All the materials were originally written in Hebrew—"the holy tongue"—the only appropriate language, according to the Hasidim, in which to record their religious teachings.[18]

Translation is always a poor substitute for the original; however, we have attempted to present the English texts so they are both faithful to the meaning of the originals and inviting to the contemporary reader. Doing so has required us to make some difficult editorial choices. All the *hanhagot* included in this volume were originally worded in the third person, that is, "One should" or "When a person"; we have chosen to change the address to the second person—"You"—in an effort to personalize the texts, bringing the reader and the Hasidic masters into closer contact. There are certain instances in which we have had no choice but to use third-person pronouns. In such cases—both when referring to God and to human beings—we have mostly maintained the male form used by the authors. While we recognize the problematic nature of this decision, we felt that shifting the gender in the texts would be too much of an intrusion, given the traditional worldview of the Hasidic masters (limited as it may have been) on this matter. However, in crafting our own reflections and comments on the texts, we have made every effort to use gender-inclusive language.

Another issue we faced was translating the few key terms and phrases that the Hasidic masters use to convey a variety of theological ideas and mystical experiences (i.e., *deveikut* = awareness of God, longing or cleaving to God, unification with God). This repetition is the result of the Rebbes' desire to create a sense of continuity between their teachings and those of the inherited tradition. To assist the contemporary reader in gaining a fuller understanding of the intent and subtlety of this material, we have chosen to use a wider variety of English words to explain these terms based on the context and spirit of each selection. Therefore, you will find certain key expressions translated differently throughout the book (i.e., *kavannah* = intention, focus, inner direction).[19]

We have also chosen to present individual texts in a poetic style, with stanzas, line breaks, and other familiar literary conventions.[20] This is not how these texts traditionally appear in print. The *hanhagot* are generally listed numerically or alphabetically, with short breaks between instructions. We have formatted the texts differently in order to enhance their contemplative power, allowing you to savor individual words, thoughts, or images. The early Hasidic tradition was largely an oral one—Torah was transmitted from master to disciple. When disciples and editors recorded the teachings of the masters, their primary concern was the preservation of the material, not the aesthetic qualities of the text. Therefore, they did not carefully consider the visual presentation of the text and its impact on the reader's experience. While no written record can ever recreate the dynamism of a personal exchange, we have attempted to reinvigorate these teachings by creatively reorganizing their layout on the page. We hope this will be helpful to you in understanding and internalizing the teachings. For reference purposes, we have also provided a series of comments, which include explanatory notes, personal reflections, and bibliographical citations.

In order to make the texts more accessible, we have created titles for each text, and organized the materials into sections with chapter headings and brief introductions. Because the *hanhagot* were designed for regular daily use, the book begins with the experience of waking up in the morning and unfolds according to the patterns of daily life, including work, prayer, study, and interaction with friends and loved ones.

The tradition of writing *hanhagot* continues in different forms in our own day. Therefore, we have also included at the end of this volume the spiritual directives of two modern Neo-Hasidic authors: Hillel Zeitlin (1871–1942), a prolific writer, journalist, and martyr of the Warsaw Ghetto, and Arthur Green, a contemporary American scholar and theologian.[21] We describe these men as "Neo-Hasidic" rather than as Hasidic because neither of them has chosen to live in traditional Hasidic communities and neither considers himself the disciple of a specific Hasidic master. Rather, each has sought in his own way to use the teachings of Hasidism (and the Kabbalah) to create a renewed spiritual vision for himself and the larger community (much like the founders of Hasidism themselves). It is our hope that the example of these two distinguished figures will inspire others to take up the practice of writing *hanhagot*—privately or with friends and family—as a spiritual exercise.

A young Hasid was once asked why he traveled such great distances to study with the Maggid of Mezeritch. "What is it that you learn from this master that you could not learn from other teachers—is it Bible, Talmud, or mystical secrets?" Without any hesitation the Hasid responded, "I travel to Mezeritch to watch the Great Maggid tie his shoelaces."[22] The *hanhagot* are designed to serve as inspiration and guidance for study and prayer, but more important, for everyday life. While we no longer have the early masters as living examples of how to sanctify daily activities, like the tying of shoelaces, we do have their *hanhagot* to assist us in our quest for holiness. We hope that this selection of inspiring Hasidic texts helps you in some small way in your ongoing search for meaning.

Or N. Rose

Part 1
Awakening & Renewal

What is your first thought upon rising? How often is it about physical or emotional exhaustion, time pressures, or worries about the new day? Are you aware of the process of waking from sleep, or do you immediately and automatically move through a series of activities to get yourself (and your family) up and out of the house? How does the beginning of your day affect the hours that follow?

The Jewish tradition offers us the *Shaharit* (Morning) service as an opportunity for early-morning reflection. The *hanhagot* in this first section propose setting aside time for contemplation even before prayer. This is envisioned as a period of silence, dedicated to communing with God, heightening our awareness of the gift of life, and celebrating the potential of the new day.

Like many of the practices proposed by the Hasidic masters, changing our early-morning routine is not easy; at times it might even seem impossible. Yet imagine how this adjustment could reshape your day. How might your morning unfold if your first thoughts were devoted to what is most significant in your life?

Sleep is often spoken of in the Jewish tradition as a foreshadowing of death. In several of the early morning prayers—*Modeh Ani, Asher Yatzar,* and *Elohai Neshmah*—we thank God for returning the soul and restoring the body. See Lawrence A. Hoffman, ed., *My People's Prayer Book: The Birkhot Hashachar (Morning Blessings),* Vol. 5 (Woodstock, Vt.: Jewish Lights Publishing, 2001).

The Hasidic masters often read Scriptural texts in creative and associative ways. In this case, the Rebbe of Amdur deconstructs the verse from Jeremiah, quoting just those words that support his idea. The text originally reads, "Israel is holy to the Lord, the first fruits of His harvest" (Jeremiah 2:3). Here, the master breaks off the sentence after the word "first," thus reversing the meaning of the sentence. Rather than Israel being the "first" or favorite in the eyes of God, the new reading calls on the Jew to make God his or her "first" thought upon rising.

A Meditation upon Rising

When you awake in the morning
immediately remember
that the blessed Creator has acted toward you with
  goodness and kindness,
for He has returned the soul to you (*Berakhot* 2a);
the soul that fills your whole body.

Use this thought to sanctify your mind.
As in the saying,
"Israel is holy to the Lord, first"
(Jeremiah 2:3).
This should be your first thought,
before your mind begins to stir.

It is also a new beginning for your body.
Therefore, use this moment to sanctify your physical
  senses—
sight, sound, and speech.

Before opening your eyes
draw the Creator to you—
likewise with your ears, mouth, and mind.

If you follow this practice,
all your deeds will be holy that day,
as it is written, "I foretell the end from the beginning
  (Isaiah 46:10)."

R. Hayim Heikel of Amdur, Hayim V'Hesed, #1

Jewish sages have articulated the value of *zerizut*, religious "eagerness" or "enthusiasm," in different ways. See, for example, *Pirkei Avot* 5:22: "Judah Ben Tema taught: Be bold as the leopard, swift as the eagle, fleet as the deer, mighty as the lion, to perform the will of your Father in heaven." In our text, the enthusiasm of the devotee has a specifically mystical inflection: just as God is the creator of multiple worlds, say the kabbalists, the human being (created in "God's image") also has the power to give birth to whole "worlds" through his or her creative efforts.

Creative Awakening

Embrace the trait of *zerizut* [eagerness, enthusiasm].

Rise from your sleep eagerly
because you have been renewed and have become a
   different person.
You are capable of bringing forth worlds,
like the Holy Blessed One ...

Tzava'at HaRivash, #20

The term *Hokhmah* ("Wisdom") is used as a technical term by the kabbalists to refer to the moment in the creation of the cosmos (and all other creative ventures) when the Divine manifests as a single spark of creative energy. The Hasidic masters often describe *Hokhmah* as the first (many earlier kabbalists see it as the second) of a series of emanations in which God takes on the garb of an endless array of creative shapes and forms. The mystics envision this process as involving ten primary emanations, called *sefirot* (singular, *sefirah*, meaning "number," often visualized by the Kabbalists as spheres), from which all of creation issues forth. The Hasidic masters write most extensively about the *sefirot* of *Hokhmah* and *Malkhut* ("Kingship" or Shekhinah, the tenth sphere), seeing them as the basic symbols of God's transcendence and immanence.

The expression *"sovev u'memaleh,"* "surrounds and fills," gives voice to this theological belief. God is imagined as a figure or force that stands above and beyond creation and is simultaneously the very stuff of creation. Scholars of religion refer to this theological perspective as panentheism. Unlike the pantheism of the seventeenth-century philosopher Benedict Spinoza, the kabbalists assert that God is not only the totality of creation, but also the initiator and active sustainer of this process. This is articulated in the oft-cited rabbinic saying, "God is the place of the world, but the world is not His place" (*Bereshit Rabbah* 68:9).

Knowing God

The first principle of faith is that God exists.

He was first, and He created all things, above and
   below—
His creations are without end.

All began with a single point—the point of Supernal
   Wisdom, *Hokhmah*.

The power of the Creator is present in all His
   creations—
God's wisdom suffuses everything that exists.

This is the meaning of the verse:
"Wisdom gives life to those who possess it"
   (Ecclesiastes 7:12).

Believe with complete faith that God fills and
   surrounds all worlds,
He is both within and beyond them all ...

R. Menahem Nahum of Chernobyl, Hanhagot Yesharot

One of the innovations of Beshtian Hasidism was the limitation placed on asceticism. As mentioned briefly in the Introduction to this volume, there were many Jewish mystics prior to the Ba'al Shem Tov (and after him) who believed that one had to follow a regimen of harsh asceticism in order to live a proper spiritual existence. While the Hasidic masters did not completely do away with asceticism, they emphasized the positive role that the body can play in a joyful religious life.

Healthy Body, Healthy Soul

Citing Rabbi Israel ben Eliezer, the Ba'al Shem Tov:
When your body is ailing, your soul is also weakened,
And you are unable to serve God properly,
Even if you are free from sin.

Therefore, guard the health of your body very carefully.

Tzava'at HaRivash, #106

Bathing in a *mikveh* (ritual bath) was (and continues to be) a regular part of the ritual life of the Hasidim. Many devotees perform morning ablutions before prayer. In traditional, non-Hasidic Jewish communities, the *mikveh* is used most often by married women, who immerse in it each month after the end of their period of menstrual bleeding, before engaging in sexual relations with their husbands. The use of *mikveh* by women and men in non-Orthodox communities is a growing phenomenon, as increasing numbers of people seek to reclaim, and reshape, ancient religious rituals. See Naomi Marmon, "Reflections on Contemporary Miqveh Practice," in *Women and Water: Menstruation in Jewish Life and Law,* Rahel R. Wasserfall, editor (Hanover, N.H.: Brandeis University/New England University Press, 1999), pp. 232–254.

The fast spoken of in this and the following text are not the statutory fasts of Yom Kippur, the Ninth of Av (marking the destruction of the Temple in Jerusalem), or other communal commemorations, but personal fasts taken on voluntarily by the individual practitioner.

Waters of Renewal

You can ascend to a high spiritual level
through regular immersion in a ritual bath *[mikveh]*.

This practice is superior to fasting,
because fasting weakens the body in its service to
God.

Better that the strength you would use fasting be
dedicated to prayer,
so that you can pray with all of your energy and
focus.

Then you will surely reach your intended goal.

R. Dov Baer of Mezeritch, Hayim V'Hesed, #20

One of the interesting ironies of Hasidism is that even as it invested great (even superhuman) power in the hands of its leaders, it also called on its adherents to take increased responsibility for their own spiritual lives. As this text makes clear, the Hasid must constantly examine himself, determining what personal practices he should undertake in order to refine his soul.

Know Your Soul

If you feel a desire to fast,
be careful not to ignore it.

Know, however,
that it is better to serve God with joy than with
     fasting,
because fasting causes sadness.

Nonetheless,
only you know if you need to fast—
if your soul requires this kind of adjustment.

Remember:
You may need to be very careful about certain
     practices—
placing great limitations upon yourself
that others do not need.

Tzava'at HaRivash, #56

The role of silence in Hasidic spirituality is discussed at length in this book's final section, In Speech & In Silence, pp. 113–131.

The Importance of Silence

Do not speak at all of everyday matters
—not even of important concerns—
from the time you get out of bed in the morning
until one hour after prayer
—not even with your spouse or children—
unless it is urgent.

Even then, be as brief as possible.

Avoid idle chatter all day long.
Restrict your conversation, say only what is needed
for your livelihood or other essential matters.
As the sages said (*Yoma* 19b):
"'Speak words of Torah' (Deuteronomy 6:4–9),
but do not indulge in worthless conversation."

Idle talk is obviously forbidden at a time when you
    could be studying Torah.
But even when you cannot study,
cleave to the blessed Creator;
do not let your attention wander from Him,
    God forbid....

R. *Mehahem Mendel of Vitebsk*, Likkutei Amarim, *#13*

Following in the footsteps of the sages of the Talmud (*Berakhot* 30b), the Hasidic masters placed great emphasis on the importance of preparation for prayer. In this case, the early Rabbis use the Scriptural verse from Amos to emphasize the need for proper physical preparation before prayer. The Rebbe from Chernobyl, however, focuses on the need for spiritual preparation.

Soul Searching before Prayer

Consider your behavior before you pray, and then
  repent.
Humble your heart by reflecting on your own
  limitations.

In doing so, you will prepare your soul
to receive God's awesome presence
as you stand before Him ready to pray.

This is the meaning of the verse,
"Prepare to meet your God, O Israel"
(Amos 4:12).

R. Menahem Nahum of Chernobyl, Hanhagot Yesharot

On the connection between prayer and ethical behavior, the modern Jewish theologian Abraham Joshua Heschel (1907–1972) wrote:

> Prayer is no panacea, no substitute for action. It is rather, like a beam thrown from a flashlight before us into the darkness. It is in this light that we grope, stumble, and climb, discover where we stand, what surrounds us, and the course which we should choose. Prayer makes visible the right, and reveals what is hampering and false. In this radiance, we behold the worth of our efforts, the range of our hopes, and the meaning of our deeds. (*Man's Quest for God* [New York: Charles Scribner's Sons, 1954], p. 8)

It is the custom of many Jewish prayer communities to collect *tzedakah* during the three daily services.

Tefilah and Tzedakah

Give as much charity [tzedakah] as you can afford.

As it is written,
"You establish Me in righteousness [tzedek]"
(i.e., through tzedakah, Isaiah 54:14).

How good it is to have a box for charity
and to place three coins in it (or at least one)
before each of the daily prayers and also before
    you eat.

        R. Menahem Nahum of Chernobyl, Hanhagot Yesharot

Part II
Prayer

The Hasidic masters devoted much of their creative energy to the subject of prayer, viewing it as the heart of the spiritual life, the source that enlivens and nourishes all other activities. The *hanhagot* on prayer focus largely on the individual worshiper, providing advice on how to develop more effective strategies for meaningful prayer experiences. The central issue that the *hanhagot* grapple with is how to use the tools of prayer—its words, letters, melodies, and periods of silence—to connect with God.

The questions raised by the early Hasidic masters remain relevant for worshipers today: How does the timing of our prayers help or hinder our awareness of the Divine? What thoughts or emotions are most beneficial to this experience, and how do we evoke them when needed? What is the connection of the body and physical movement to prayer? How do we deal with failure—inconsistency and distractions—in cultivating our prayer lives?

The Rabbis of the Talmud engage in lengthy discussions about the precise timing of the three daily prayers—*Shaharit* (Morning service), *Minhah* (Afternoon service), and *Ma'ariv* (Evening service). These services are designed to link one's prayer life to the natural cycles of day and night (*Berakhot* 1a). As the verse in Psalms states, "Evening and morning and at noon will I pray and cry aloud, and He will hear my voice" (55:17).

Sensitive to the impact of the light of the sun on the experience of morning prayer, the Besht urges the worshiper to begin praying the *Shaharit* (from the root *shahar,* "dawn") before sunrise. Using the mythical imagery of the Kabbalah, he describes this liminal time as being free from the "angels of wrath" (celestial or psychological), who make their appearance with the harsh rays of the sun.

Prayer before Dawn

Recite your morning prayers before sunrise,
both in summer and winter.

The difference between the time before and after
    sunrise
is as great as the distance between east and west.

Prior to sunrise you can still negate all harsh judgments.

This is alluded to in the verse,
"The sun is like a groom coming forth from his bridal
    chamber, rejoicing like a warrior,
and nothing is hidden from its heat [hamato]"
(Psalms 19: 6–7).

The Hebrew word hamato [its heat] can also be read
    as heimato [its wrath],
meaning once the sun rises over the earth,
you cannot avoid the harsh judgments of the angels of
    wrath.

This matter is not to be taken lightly.

The Ba'al Shem Tov was so careful about this practice
that if he did not have a minyan [prayer quorum] by
    sunrise,
he would pray alone.

                              Tzava'at HaRivash, #16

THE UNFOLDING OF *TEFILAH* [PRAYER]

This teaching articulates the Hasidic understanding of prayer as a journey. The goal is not to recite a maximum of words in a minimum of time. Nor is prayer presented here as an opportunity to make requests of God. The purpose of *tefilah* is to encounter the Divine as fully and intimately as possible. This meeting does not happen instantly, but takes time and care, like any romantic courtship. The Hasidic masters instruct us to be patient, slowly building our strength as the journey unfolds.

The Unfolding of Tefilah [Prayer]

When praying,
move gradually.

Do not exhaust all of your strength at the outset.

Rather, begin slowly,
and in the midst of your prayer,
cleave to God with greater intensity.

Then you will even be able to recite the words of
    prayer very quickly
without losing your focus.

While you may be unable to connect with God at the
    beginning of prayer,
continue to recite your words with attention and
    focus.

Strengthen yourself
step by step,
until God helps you to pray more intensely.

Tzava'at HaRivash, #32

The Jewish mystical tradition is replete with sexual imagery. In attempting to describe the ineffable experience of unity with the Divine, the mystics use metaphors that are most powerful to them and their disciples. In this case, the adept is instructed to pay close attention to his movements in prayer. The traditional swaying motion of prayer is here understood as the rhythm of lovemaking between the human worshiper and the Divine. Like their kabbalistic forebears, the Hasidic masters understood that religious and sexual passions have a common source and share many of the same qualities. Because these teachings were written by male teachers for their male disciples, this text (and many like it) focuses on the experience of a (heterosexual) male at prayer, encountering the Shekhinah, the feminine, indwelling Divine presence.

The Shekhinah, the tenth *sefirah* (see the note on "Knowing God," p. 6), is imagined by the Hasidim as an immanent force with whom the mystic can unite in moments of contemplation or ecstasy. It is only when the Hasid becomes aware of the Divine source of his passions that he can truly consummate the relationship and stand as one with the Shekhinah.

The Eros of Prayer

Prayer is coupling *[zivug]* with the Shekhinah.

Just as there is motion at the beginning of sexual
    coupling,
so too must you sway at the beginning of prayer.

Then, be still—
at one with the Shekhinah.

Your swaying will lead you to an intense spiritual
    arousal:
This should cause you to ask:
"Why am I moving my body?—
it is because the Shekhinah is standing before me."
This awareness will bring you to great rapture
    [hitlahavut].

Tzava'at HaRivash, #68

The Hasidic masters write a great deal about the challenges of prayer and the inevitable obstacles one faces in such experiences. In this context, they often speak of the *kelipot* as the forces of evil that tempt and distract, keeping us from meeting God. The concept of the *kelipot* (singular, *kelipah*), however, predates Hasidism by several centuries. It is first used by Jewish mystics in the early medieval period, and is then reconceived by the sixteenth-century mystic Isaac Luria (1534–1572). Arthur Green explains the Lurianic conception of the *kelipot* as follows:

> Luria claimed that creative energy, in the form of divine light, was sent into this newly emanated world from the mysterious core of divinity. The light was contained in certain "vessels." The emanated world was not sufficiently holy to contain God's light, however, so the vessels smashed and the sparks of light were scattered. The broken shards of the vessels, which are now called *kelipot,* cover those sparks or keep the divine light hidden. As such, they become active enemies of those who seek light however, in the sixteenth century. (*These Are the Words: A Vocabulary of Jewish Spiritual Life* [Woodstock, Vt.: Jewish Lights Publishing, 1999], p. 16)

It is Luria's depiction of the *kelipot* that most informs the Hasidic understanding of this term.

The Word: Body and Soul

There is "a flaming sword that revolves around the
  Garden of Eden,
guarding the path to the Tree of Life" (Genesis 3:24).

When you wish to join your thoughts to the upper
  worlds
—to the blessed Creator—
the *kelipot* [forces of evil] may block you from doing so.

Nonetheless, in spite of all obstacles, force yourself,
  over and over again
—even within the space of a single prayer—
to cleave to God ...

At first, say the "body" of the word,
and then invest it with its "soul."

Likewise, when you first begin to pray,
rouse yourself through your body
—use all your physical strength—
to allow the power of your soul to shine through.

Thus it is written in the *Zohar* (III:166b, 168a),
"Logs that will not burn should be splintered;
then they will light."

After this, you will be able to worship with just your
  mind,
without any need for bodily movement.

Tzava'at HaRivash, #58

Our experience of separation, says the Maggid, is an illusion created by God to give us the opportunity to make the great discovery of unity as independent seekers. In this text, R. Dov Baer calls on the worshiper to focus his attention not on the meaning of the prayers, but on the letters. Like prior mystics, he believed that the letters of the Hebrew alphabet possess inherent spiritual power. This is based on the biblical notion that God created the world through speech (Genesis I: "And God *said,* Let there be light"). In deconstructing the words of prayer, by stripping them down to their component parts, one can experience the presence of the Divine within the letters themselves.

Removing the Veil

Use the words you utter in prayer
as tools to break through the partition
that separates you from the Divine,
until you are able to cleave to God.

Know that each and every letter of the alphabet
comes from an open and endless world above,
and every letter that leaves your mouth in prayer
awakens these worlds.

Therefore, utter the words of your prayer
with passion, joy, and a feeling of intimacy with the
    Divine.

R. Dov Baer of Mezeritch, Hayim V'Hesed, #5

This text, like many others in Hasidism, stresses the instrumental nature of Jewish ritual. The goal of prayer is to connect to God; the *siddur* (prayer book) is a precious tool—a compass or guidebook—with which to reach this goal. However, if we find that reading the words of the *siddur* is distracting or limiting, we are instructed to close our eyes and turn inward.

Eyes Open or Closed

When you are on a low spiritual level,
pray out of a prayer book;
looking at the letters will allow you to pray with
   kavannah [focus].

When you are attached to the Supernal world,
   however,
it is better to close your eyes,
so that your sight does not distract you
from connecting to God.

Tzava'at HaRivash, *#40*

The paradoxical idea that we need God's help to pray (to God!) is articulated in the introduction to the *Amidah* (the "standing" prayer): "Open my lips, O Lord, so that I may speak Your praise" (Psalms 51:17).

Kavannah literally means "direction." It is used throughout the Jewish tradition to refer to religious focus or concentration (*kavannat ha-lev*, "directing the heart"). The goal is to perform all our rituals and deeds with proper *kavannah*. Although many medieval kabbalists used this word as a technical term for the detailed mystical meditations *(kavannot)* they created, the Hasidim mostly return to the older, simpler meaning of this expression.

The *Aleinu* (named after its opening word, "It is incumbent upon us") is one of the oldest prayers (second or third century C.E.) in the Jewish tradition and since the fourteenth century has served as the closing hymn to the three daily services.

The Gift of Inner Focus

It is impossible to pray with *kavannah* [focus] without
    support.
Therefore, you must ask God for help.

Consider it a great gift when God helps you to focus
even for half of the *tefilah* [prayer].

If, toward the end, you feel weak and your *kavannah*
    is lost,
so be it—what can you do?

Simply pray to the best of your ability
—even if less intensely—
until the end of *Aleinu* [the closing hymn].

Tzava'at HaRivash, #60–61

The notion that God is hidden (or hides) from human beings is explored in a number of different ways in Hasidism (as previously discussed in "Removing the Veil," p. 30). In many cases, the Hasidic masters teach that it is we who cause this situation through our spiritual blindness (we are both the observer and the King's soldiers). They insist that if we search for God with openness and purity of heart, we will discover the Divine waiting for us with open arms. The following teaching, attributed to the Ba'al Shem Tov, is one of the most well-known Hasidic formulations of this idea:

> Once there was a very wise king who created illusory walls, towers, and gates, and he commanded his subjects to approach him through these gates and towers. He also instructed that the riches of the kingdom be dispersed at every gate. There were those who reached the first gate, took the riches, and left [there were others who journeyed farther, but no one reached the king] ... until the king's one and only son bravely decided to go directly to his father, the king. The son realized that there was nothing separating him from his father, that it was all an illusion.
>
> The Holy Blessed One hides in a number of garments and behind [many] partitions, and as it is known, "God's glory fills the whole earth" [Isaiah 6:3], and every movement and thought, everything, comes from God....There is no separation between man and God. (*Keter Shem Tov*, edited by R. Aaron ben Tzvi Hirsch of Apta. Zolkiev: 1794).

Divine Hide & Seek

Do not say:
"I will pray when I am able to do so with great
  hitlahavut [enthusiasm, rapture],
but otherwise I will not force myself to pray."

On the contrary!

This matter is comparable to a king who changes his
  garments when waging war.
Those who are familiar with the king
recognize him by his gestures and mannerisms.
Those who are unfamiliar with him
discover the king's location by watching his soldiers,
and observing what they guard most carefully.

So, too, if you are unable to pray,
understand that the "King" is being guarded from
  you.
Thus, redouble your efforts,
for the King present,
even if He is in hiding.

                              Tzava'at HaRivash, #86

It is somewhat surprising that the Great Maggid describes the experience of individual prayer as being more conducive to *deveikut* ("closeness to God") than communal prayer, since most rabbinic authorities favor group prayer. In fact, according to Jewish law there are certain parts of the liturgy that can only be recited with a minyan, a "quorum" of ten adults (ten men in Orthodox tradition). This includes such central prayers as the *Barekhu* (the call to prayer), the *Kaddish* (the memorial prayer for the dead), and the Torah service. This is one of many Hasidic texts that attempts to address the tension between the spiritual needs of the individual and the need to follow the tradition.

Individual Prayer

It is easier to connect to God
when praying alone
than when praying with others.

Therefore, when you are alone, be happy—
for joy is necessary for achieving *deveikut* [closeness
  to God].

In truth, you should be just as close to the Creator
  throughout the day,
as you are in prayer.
The only difference is that during prayer
you are in a more expansive state than during the
  rest of the day.

> *R. Dov Baer of Mezeritch*, Hayim V'Hesed, #5

Part III
Preparation for Daily Life

One of the central teachings of the Hasidic masters is that our relationship to God is not limited to the synagogue, the house of study, or other formal "religious" activities. The doctrine of *avodah be'gashmiut* (service through the physical) posits that if approached with proper awareness, every moment can be an opportunity to serve the Divine.

One of the innovations of the early Hasidic masters was making such experiences available to large numbers of people, not just the dedicated few who choose to live *vita contemplativa*—a life of uninterrupted mystical contemplation. Rather, the *hanhagot* encourage us to discover the Divine within the natural flow of our lives—while traveling, working, or spending time with family and friends.

The message of *avodah be'gashmiut* may be difficult for us to internalize, living as we do in a society that carefully upholds the separation between religion and state, relegating most religious activities to institutional settings or private gatherings. In the minds of the Hasidic masters, however, all of life is "religious": God desires our service *(avodah)* in all that we do. The texts in this section challenge us to re-imagine our lives, seeking ways to discover the Divine in all aspects of life.

This visualization exercise might seem strange because of the Maggid's instruction to envision God in your mind's eye. This would appear to contradict various statements in the Bible forbidding us from seeing God or creating visual representations of the Divine.

In truth, the Bible is far from consistent on this matter. Moses, we are told, encountered God "face to face" (Exodus 33:11; Deuteronomy 34:10), and the prophet Ezekiel had a vision of the Divine in which he saw the "likeness of a man" sitting upon a throne and chariot (1:26–28). Jewish mystics have dealt with this tension in different ways. In some cases, they focus their creative efforts on hearing the voice of God. However, more commonly, the kabbalists affirm the Bible's ruling against the creation of graven images or idols, while simultaneously developing detailed techniques to envision the Divine in their minds. By restricting this activity to the imagination, the mystics are able to uphold the commandment against creating visual representations of God, while also allowing themselves the freedom to imaginatively enrich their spiritual lives. For a scholarly treatment of the subject of vision and imagination in medieval Kabbalah, see Elliot R. Wolfson, *Through a Speculum that Shines* (Princeton, N.J.: Princeton University Press, 1994). Louis Jacobs has collected and translated a series of Jewish mystical testimonials of different kinds in *The Jewish Mystics* (London: Schocken Books, 1976).

Mirror Images

It is a great achievement
to be able to envision the Creator in your mind's eye
    at all times—
as if you were looking at another person.

Imagine that God is also looking at you,
just as another person would look at you.

Maintain this vision in clear and pure thought.

Contemplate the Creator's glory,
which "fills the whole earth" (Isaiah 6:3).

Remind yourself that God is the master of all things in
    the world,
and can fulfill all the desires of your heart.
Therefore, He is the only one worthy of your trust.

Understand that just as you look at physical objects,
you must also look with your mind's eye at the
    Shekhinah [God's indwelling presence].
She is forever with you ...

"When you walk, She will lead you, and when you lie
    down, She will watch over you" (Proverbs 6:22).

R. Dov Baer of Mezeritch, Hayim V'Hesed, #10

In its original context, the verse from Leviticus (21:12) speaks about the prohibition against the High Priest leaving the grounds of the Tabernacle (the portable Temple in the wilderness). In many Hasidic teachings the Temple is no longer viewed as a physical entity, but rather as a description of distinct states of consciousness in which one feels most intimately connected to the Divine. Prayer and meditation are viewed as ideal vehicles for "pilgrimage" to this inner shrine. The question raised in this text is what to do when life demands that we journey away from the Temple. How do we ensure that we will return home?

Divine Homecoming

Attach yourself to the Creator with complete love.
This love must surpass your love for any worldly good,
because everything is rooted in the Divine.

Repeat the following statement:
"I want to do God's will, to cause Him joy,
and to worship Him without interruption."

Attach yourself to the Upper World—to the Divine.

This is the hidden meaning of the verse,
"And from the Temple he will not exit"
(Leviticus 21:12).

When you have an everyday need,
remember that you are moving downward from the
    Upper World.

Imagine that you are like a person who leaves his home,
but wants to return as soon as possible.
As this person journeys, he is constantly asking himself,
"When will I return home?"
You, too, must constantly think of returning to the
    Upper World.

Remember: your true home is with the blessed
    Creator.

R. Dov Baer of Mezeritch, Hayim V'Hesed, *#1*

Deveikut, literally "cleaving" or "attachment," is a key term in the Jewish mystical tradition. While in medieval Kabbalah the term usually refers to an intense experience of unification with the Divine, in Hasidism it is also used more broadly to refer to awareness of God. Achieving *deveikut*—in its various forms—is the ultimate goal of Hasidism. See Gershom Scholem, "*Deveikut* or Communion with God," and Ada Rapoport-Albert, "God and the *Tzaddik* as the Two Focal Points of Hasidic Worship," both reprinted in *Essential Papers on Hasidism,* edited by Gershon David Hundert (New York: New York University Press, 1991), pp. 275–298 and pp. 299–329.

Spiritual Practice

Attach yourself to the blessed Creator,
and in that state of *deveikut* [connection to God]
pray for some household need ...
even though there is no immediate need for it.

Do this in order to train yourself
to keep your mind connected to the blessed Creator,
even when it comes to mundane matters.

This practice will help you
maintain your *deveikut* at all times.

Tzava'at HaRivash, *#81*

The notion that God has needs that only humankind can fulfill is addressed in detail in medieval Kabbalah. In most cases, these discussions focus on the mystical power of the ritual mitzvot (commandments), and the ways in which one can bring joy and wholeness to God through their intentional fulfillment. This *hanhagah* (like many Hasidic teachings) introduces the notion that God also needs our service in the world, through interaction with others.

Many Paths to God

Serve God in all you do ...

There will be times when you are engaged in
   conversation,
and you will be unable to study Torah.
At such times,
join yourself to God internally ...

This is also the case when you travel
and cannot pray or study as you usually do.
At such times, serve God in other ways.

Do not be upset by this,
because God needs us to serve Him in all that
   we do ...

This is why He presented you with the opportunity
   to travel
or to speak with other people;
it is so that you may serve Him in these particular ways.

R. Dov Baer of Mezeritch, Hayim V'Hesed, *#19*

King Solomon is described in the Bible and in rabbinic literature as a person of unparalleled wisdom. Following on earlier rabbinic and kabbalistic traditions, King Solomon is introduced in our text as a model of mystical wisdom: he is able to discern the presence of the Divine in all that he encounters. For a sampling of rabbinic legends on King Solomon, see *The Book of Legends,* edited by Hayim Nahman Bialik and Yehoshua Hana Ravnitzky, and translated by William G. Braude (New York: Schocken Books, 1992), p. 123.

King Solomon's Example

Pay close attention to everything that happens,
everything you hear or see,
but especially to what you do.

This is why it is written of King Solomon
that he "spoke about the trees" (I Kings 5:13)—
meaning, all that he saw led him to serve God.

Everything in the world is needed for God's worship
—whether pure or impure—
because everything is God;
His guidance and providence are cloaked in Creation.

R. *Dov Baer of Mezeritch*, Hanhagot Tzaddikim

The phrase "sweetened at the root" expresses the belief that everything in life emanates from the Divine. Therefore, even the most difficult moments of existence can be uplifted and redeemed. This is achieved, says the Maggid, by maintaining your consciousness (remaining "wholehearted in your devotion") of the Divine origin of all life and mentally elevating each experience to its root above.

As this text makes clear, the Hasidic masters sought to instill in their disciples an awareness of the Divine that would guide them in all aspects of life. The Rebbes knew that because the Hasidim lived such highly regimented ritual lives, their religious practice was at risk of devolving into mere routine. It is this concern that the Maggid addresses in the final line of this text. This issue is discussed at length in the fifth section of this volume, Torah Study & Mitzvot, pp. 89–112.

The Power of the Human Mind

If you should ask me,
"Is it possible to use my mind to uplift all of creation
so that it is 'sweetened in its root'?"
I would respond,
"You must be wholehearted with YHVH your God"
(Deuteronomy 18:13).

Just remain wholehearted in your thoughts of God,
and your pure thoughts will ascend in an instant....

If you want to climb a ladder,
you cannot immediately reach the top from the
      bottommost rung;
you must climb gradually.

However, when you speak to God or contemplate His
      greatness,
you can ascend directly from the bottommost rung of
consciousness to the top....

If you carry out all of your actions thoughtfully,
You will immediately stand in the presence of God.

This awareness will keep your religious practice from
      turning into rote actions.

R. Dov Baer of Mezeritch, Hayim V'Hesed, *#17*

In Lurianic Kabbalah (sixteenth century), it is believed that every creation—animate and inanimate—contains sparks of Divine light (for more on the "sparks," see the note on the text "The Word: Body and Soul," p. 28). It is also believed that every creation derives from a specific realm within the Godhead. Human souls have a special affinity—a "root" connection—with all other creations that emanate from its place of origin. It is, therefore, incumbent on every person to restore the fallen sparks that emanate from his or her particular "soul root."

Holy Sparks

"The Torah is concerned about Israel's livelihood"
(*Yoma* 39a).

Why is this so?

In making use of your clothing, food, and other
   physical objects
seek to derive benefit from the Divine force inherent
   in each of these things.

For without this essential vitality, nothing could exist.
Further, recognize that these objects contain "holy
   sparks"
that relate directly to the root of your soul.

I have heard that this is why one person may love
   something
and another may hate it.

Therefore, when you eat or make use of an object
—even if for a physical need—
you can restore the sparks in that object.
They are restored when you use the strength
—given to you by the garment, the food, or any other
   object—
to serve God.

When you have restored all the sparks that relate to
   your soul's root,
God takes the object from you and gives it to another.
He does so because the remaining sparks relate to that
   person's soul.

Tzava'at HaRivash, *#109*

The message of acceptance and submission articulated in this text stands in sharp contrast to the following well-known Hasidic text, "The Kaddish of R. Levi Isaac of Berditchev" (d. 1810):

Good morning to You, Lord, Master of the Universe.
I, Levi Yitzhak, son of Sarah of Berditchev,
I come to You with a *Din Torah* [legal suit] from Your people Israel.

What do You want of Your people Israel?
What have You demanded of Your people Israel?
For everywhere I look it says, "Say to the Children of Israel,"
And every other verse says, "Speak to the Children of Israel,"
And over and over, "Command the Children of Israel."

Father, sweet Father in Heaven,
How many nations are there in the world?
Persians, Babylonians, Edomites.

The Russians, what do they say?
That their Czar is the only ruler.
The Prussians, what do they say?
That their Kaiser is supreme.
And the English, what do they say?
That George III is the sovereign.

(continued)

Preparing for Hard Times

Every day a new challenge will come your way—
be it curses, insults, or monetary crises.

Make sure you are prepared for these experiences
    before they unfold.

Then you will be able to accept everything with
    happiness
and not rebel against God in your pain,
enduring faithfully all the trials and tribulations that
    are visited upon you.

R. Hayim Heikel of Amdur, Hayim V'Hesed, #14

And I, Levi Yitzhak, son of Sarah of Berditchev say,
"*Yisgadal v'yiskadash shmei raboh—*
Magnified and sanctified is Thy name."

And I, Levi Yitzhak, son of Sarah of Berditchev, say,
"From my stand I will not waver,
And from my place I will not move
Until there be an end to this.
Yisgadal v'yiskadash shmei raboh—

Magnified and sanctified is only Your name."

This translation is from Samuel H. Dresner, *Levi Yitzhak of Berditchev: Portrait of a Hasidic Master* (New York: Hartmore House, 1974), p. 86. See p. 60 for further discussion of the issue of spiritual submission in Hasidism.

Part IV
Personal & Interpersonal Conduct

Awareness of the holiness of all life cultivated through the practice of *avodah be'gashmiut* (service through the physical) undoubtedly influences our attitudes and behavior. Similarly, the Hasidic masters believed that our daily conduct can profoundly affect our relationship with God. The *hanhagot* in this section are designed to assist us in living out the teaching of Divine immanence in our personal and interpersonal lives.

As in the previous sections, the texts are direct and concrete: They address such common challenges as overcoming anger and greed, cultivating equanimity, letting go of unrealistic expectations, and changing negative habits. They teach compassion and kindness to self and others in the context of a mystical theology that proclaims that all of life is Divine.

There is an ongoing tension in Hasidism about how best to serve God in the world. Is this accomplished by assuming an activist approach, by working to shape our lives independently, even in moments of pain or sadness? Or is it preferable to cultivate a more passive, accepting attitude, seeing the events of life as a series of Divine decrees? The Hasidic masters do not propose one single solution to this dilemma, but rather approach it differently depending on the circumstance. As the Israeli scholar Rivka Schatz-Uffenheimer wrote, "Hasidism knew how to live with the paradoxes within itself, with simultaneous feelings of intense mission and a tendency to negation and non-activity, so that the boundaries between things are not always clear." See *Hasidism as Mysticism: Quietistic Elements in Eighteenth-Century Hasidic Thought,* translated by Jonathan Chipman (Jerusalem: Magnes Press and Princeton, N.J.: Princeton University Press, 1993), p. 58.

Divine Surrender

"Leave all to God" (Psalms 37:5).

Plant this idea so firmly in your mind
that you respond to everything in life by saying,
"This is from God."

Ask God to bring you what He thinks you need,
because He knows what is good for you;
even though this may not be what you think is best
   for you.

Give over all of your needs to God.

This is the meaning of the verse:
"Cast your burden on YHVH and He will sustain
   you" (Psalms 55:23).

R. Dov Baer of Mezeritch, Hayim V'Hesed, *#20–21*

The terms *din* (judgment) and *hesed* (loving-kindness) are basic to the Jewish mystical vocabulary. *Hesed* expresses God's boundless love for all creation. *Din* is the attribute that offsets this tendency by introducing a measure of restraint or control (even love requires boundaries). While both are needed for a balanced existence, the Hasidic masters insist that God prefers to tip the scales in favor of *hesed*. It is we, however, who ultimately determine which of these forces will dominate our lives.

Creating Your Own Reality

"He who trusts in YHVH
will be surrounded by loving-kindness [hesed]"
   (Psalms 32:10).

However, if you behave in the opposite manner
—if you are always afraid of harsh Divine
   judgments—
then you will attach yourself to this harshness
and evil will befall you, heaven forbid.
As it is written, "To bring on them the very thing
   they dread" (Isaiah 66:4).

Your thoughts determine your reality ...

Therefore, absorb yourself in thoughts of God.

R. Dov Baer of Mezeritch, Hayim V'Hesed, #23

Another important pair of terms in Hasidism is *ahavah* (love) and *yirah* (fear or awe). These emotions are viewed as the two primary human responses to the Divine (mirroring God's basic modes of interaction with us). As one might expect, the Rebbes tend to favor the response of *ahavah* over *yirah*. However, when speaking about the importance of *yirah*, they encourage their disciples to develop a sense of *yirah* that is born out of awe and reverence for God, and not out of fear of punishment or retribution.

True Fear

"The fear of the Lord is His treasure" (Isaiah 33:6).

... There are different types of fear to be sure,
but the true treasure is awe before God's greatness—
fearing Him because He is master and ruler,
the Source of all worlds.

It is this attitude that will lead you to serve God with
    all your strength and devotion.
You will do so not out of fear of death, punishment,
    or hell;
these will all be meaningless in the face of your true
    awe before the Creator.

R. Menahem Nahum of Chernobyl, Hanhagot Yesharot

Rabbi Shimon bar Yohai (RaShbY), the famed second-century sage, became the archetypal mystic in Judaism after the appearance of the Zohar in thirteenth-century Spain, which was attributed to him by its disseminator (and more than likely its chief author), Moses ben Shem Tov De Leon (1240–1305). For more on this subject, see Daniel C. Matt, *Zohar: Annotated & Explained* (Woodstock, Vt.: SkyLight Paths Publishing, 2002).

The Talmudic source quoted here (*Berakhot* 35b) discourages people from following RaShbY's model of life, dedicated exclusively to Torah study without any work in the world. Our author, however, rereads this text as a warning against the dangers of serving the ego in the spiritual quest.

Do Not Reach for Spiritual Heights

"Many attempted to act like Rabbi Shimon bar Yohai,
but failed" (*Berakhot* 35b).

The meaning of this statement is as follows:
These people performed many acts of self-
    mortification
in an attempt to reach the great heights of bar Yohai.
That is why they failed.

When serving God, think only about pleasing the
    blessed Creator,
and not about reaching great heights.

Tzava'at HaRivash, #47

One hears in this text an echo of the conflicts between the Hasidim and the Mitnaggedim. One of the major sources of tension was the Mitnaggedic claim that the Hasidim were too wild and unruly during prayer—often starting late in the morning (beyond the prescribed time) and singing and dancing for hours (and thus neglecting Torah study). While in this text the Hasidim are urged to respond to such criticism with silence, maintaining their equanimity, history demonstrates that the Hasidic-Mitnaggedic conflicts involved harsh polemics from both sides (see note 7 to the Introduction on p. 148).

The Humble Way

When people ridicule you about your worship
—whether about your style of prayer or other
     matters—
do not respond.

Do not even respond in a positive way,
so as to avoid being drawn into a quarrel
or becoming arrogant,
which will cause you to forget the blessed Creator.

As our sages said:
"Man's silence leads him to humility"
(*Sha'arei Kedushah* II:5).

Tzava'at HaRivash, #49

Shiflut, "humility" or "lowliness," is one of the most important ethical-spiritual virtues in Hasidism. It is viewed not as a value born out of self-loathing, but as the proper response to a true understanding of God's greatness and the fragility of our lives. Paradoxically, it is by cultivating one's humility that a person can rise to great heights and have a profound impact on God and the world.

All God's Creatures

Do not say in your heart that you are better than your
   neighbor
because you worship with greater intensity then he
   does.

Remember that you, like all other creatures,
were created to worship God.
It was God who chose *not* to endow your neighbor
with the same abilities He gave you.

When you reflect on this,
you will realize that there is no reason to think that
   you are superior
even to an earthworm, let alone to another human
   being.

For like the best of humankind,
the worm serves God with all its strength and
   intelligence;
and the Torah teaches that the human being
is really as worthless *[rimah v'toleah]* as a worm
   [tola'at]:
"But I am a worm, less than man" (Psalms 22:7).

If God had not endowed you with consciousness,
you, too, would worship like a worm ...

Therefore, think of yourself, the worm, and all other
   little creatures

as companions in this world
—we are all created things—
possessing only those abilities given to us by the
blessed Creator.

Always keep this in mind.

R. Hayim Heikel of Amdur, Hayim V'Hesed, #7

This text reiterates the mystical belief in the theurgic power (the power to affect God) of human action (see the note on "Many Paths to God," p. 48). According to the mythology of Kabbalah, when we act for the good we bring harmony to the Divine, uniting the male and female aspects within the Godhead. However, when we act in negative ways, we cause a cosmic rupture, separating these forces. The ultimate goal of human action, say the kabbalists, is to bring lasting unity to God, and consequently to the world.

The Shekhinah is considered to be the most vulnerable of the *sefirot* because of Her proximity to the lower worlds of creation and the forces of evil. As a female potency, She is often depicted as a "damsel in distress" who is in need of the protection of the male devotee and the male powers of the Godhead. See Elliot K. Ginsberg, *The Sabbath in the Classical Kabbalah* (New York: State University of New York Press, 1989), pp. 26–58; and Arthur Green, *A Guide to the Zohar* (Stanford: Stanford University Press, 2003).

Arrogance Begets Anger

It is written in the Gemara (*Megilah* 28b),
"I did not become angry in my house."

At times, you may have to act as if you were angry,
instilling fear in others;
but do not do so "in your house"—
do not become angry in your body and soul.

Anger emanates from arrogance,
and even the slightest arrogant thought is
    destructive....
All your thoughts reverberate throughout the cosmos,
and your arrogance can blemish the worlds above and
    displace the Shekhinah.

As it is written,
"Every haughty person is an abomination to the
    Lord" (Proverbs 16:5).

R. Dov Baer of Mezeritch, Hayim V'Hesed, #8

On the imagery of the *kelipot* in Hasidim, see the note on "The Word: Body and Soul," p. 28.

The notion of acting "for the sake of heaven" *(l'shem shamayim)* is a rabbinic concept, applied to different areas of Jewish life. Perhaps the most well-known discussion of this issue is found in *Pirkei Avot* 5:17:

A controversy for the sake of heaven will have lasting value, but a controversy not for heaven's sake will not endure. What is an example of a controversy for the sake of heaven? The debates between Hillel and Shammai [two of the foremost early sages, first century B.C.E.]. What is an example of controversy not for heaven's sake? The rebellion of Korah and his associates [against the leadership of Moses and Aaron, Numbers 16].

Righteous Indignation

Your anger should always be for "the sake of
   heaven."
Direct your anger toward the *kelipot* [forces of evil]
in the person who upsets you,
and not at the person himself.

Understand that the *kelipot* scare him into doing evil
   things.

Then you can use your anger
to bring the *kelipot* under the sway of holiness.

R. Dov Baer of Mezeritch, Hayim V'Hesed, *#12*

The commandment to "love your neighbor as yourself" is one of the most frequently quoted maxims in the Jewish and Christian traditions. Rabbi Akiva, the great second-century sage, taught, "Love your neighbor as yourself is the most important principle of the Torah." His colleague Ben Azzai disagreed, insisting that more basic than love is the belief that all human beings are created "in the image of God" (Genesis 5:1). This classic debate is found in *Genesis Rabbah* 24.

Love Your Neighbor

Guard yourself against hating anyone,
except for truly evil people,
whom you know with certainty cannot be judged
    favorably.

However, if it is at all possible for you to judge people
    favorably,
you must try to love them—
with all your soul and all your might
(Deuteronomy 6:4),
just as you love yourself.

This is what it means to
"Love your neighbor as yourself"
(Leviticus 19:18).

        R. Elimelech of Lizensk, Noam Elimelekh, #8

Stories about hidden *tzaddikim* (righteous people) abound in Hasidism. These tales describe how the most unlikely of characters—the beggar, the woodchopper, the water carrier—turns out to be a person of great spiritual depth and superior ethical character. Already in the rabbinic period there are discussions of thirty-six *(lamed vav)* righteous individuals who sustain the world through their secret acts of kindness (*Sanhedrin* 97b, *Sukkah* 45b). The Hasidic masters often speak of the *nister* (concealed) as a *tzaddik* of a higher order than the *meforsam* (revealed). See Martin Buber's *Tales of the Hasidim* (New York: Schocken, 1975).

Concealed and Revealed Acts of Piety

Perform your acts of piety in a concealed manner,
so that people will not take notice of your deeds.

Yet, until you reach an advanced spiritual rung, act
   openly.

Otherwise, if you behave like the rest of the world
   outwardly,
and carry out your good deeds only in secret,
you may be drawn after the ways of the world
and your intention to act with integrity will lead to
   failure.

Tzava'at HaRivash, #65

KNOW WHO STANDS BEFORE YOU

Tanna de-bei Eliyahu is a collection of legends and folktales (midrashim) about biblical characters and early Rabbis. It was composed between 650 and 900 C.E.

Know Who Stands before You

"Rebuke your fellow" (Leviticus 19:17).
It is taught in *Tanna de-bei Eliyahu* (18:40):
Only rebuke a person who is a partner in Torah and
  mitzvot,
but do not rebuke those who do not follow this path.

As it is written,
"Do not reprove the scorner lest he hate you;
rebuke a wise person and he will love you"
(Proverbs 9:8).

R. Hayim Heikel of Amdur, Hayim V'Hesed, *#15*

The *tzaddik* (the "righteous one") is a synonym for Rebbe (Hasidic master) in Hasidism. The Hasidic masters were so venerated by their disciples that they were often viewed as possessing semi-Divine powers. This perception led to the development of a complex relationship between the *tzaddik* and his community. While there was great love and closeness between master and disciple, there was also a rigid power structure in which the Rebbe was viewed as the unquestioned leader of the community, beyond the reproach of the Hasidim.

Within this hierarchical context, however, Hasidism demonstrates great sensitivity to the dynamism of the spiritual life. Alternating periods of "highs" and "lows" are recognized as inevitable (or even necessary) components of mystical striving, even for the *tzaddik*.

Beware of the Glowing Coals

"Beware of their glowing coals lest you be burnt …
all their words are like fiery coals"
(*Pirkei Avot* 2:10) …

The Ba'al Shem Tov, of blessed memory, said:
A perfect *tzaddik* ["righteous person," Hasidic master]
may sometimes fall from his elevated state
and worship in *katnut* [with limited awareness];
he may not pray with great *kavannah* [inner focus],
and sometimes he may even go idle.

Seeing the *tzaddik* in this state,
you might think that you can act in a similar manner.
After all, if the saintly and pious can do so,
why can't I?

Our teacher from *Pirkei Avot* [Ethics of the Fathers]
    thus cautions:
Do not compare yourself to the Torah sage and the
    tzaddik.
For when the *tzaddik* will awaken from his "sleep"
and again pray and study as he did before,
he will elevate all of his trivial words.

You who observe him, however,
are but a simple person,
unaware of the mysteries of Divine worship.
How dare you compare yourself to the *tzaddik*?

This is the meaning of "beware of their glowing coals."

Even when *tzaddikim* fall from their heights
and act like "dimmed coals"
—uttering idle words or engaging in idle deeds—
beware!

Do not apply a lesson from their actions to your life,
for even their idle talk is like a "fiery coal."

Tzava'at HaRivash, #96

Part V
Torah Study & Mitzvot

Torah study and the fulfillment of the mitzvot (commandments) are considered the cornerstones of traditional Judaism. One might assume, however, that because the Hasidim placed such great emphasis on discovering God in all aspects of life, they may have de-emphasized the importance of traditional Jewish practice—this is not the case. The Rebbes (Hasidic masters) believed these modes of worship to be central to the spiritual quest, but reinterpreted their significance in light of a renewed focus on *kavannah* (inner intention).

The *hanhagot* in this section do not emphasize the simple fulfillment of the mitzvot, but, rather, they focus on the process of their fulfillment. The question is not *how much* you have learned, but *how* you have learned. The Hasidic masters viewed traditional Jewish rituals and practices as precious tools with which to encounter the Divine. It is not enough just to study or pray; we must be conscious of the motivations for these practices and be mindful of the ultimate goal of our actions. It is for this reason that the *hanhagot* warn us against intellectual arrogance in Torah study and self-righteousness in the fulfillment of the mitzvot.

While contemporary seekers understand the Torah and mitzvot in different and even conflicting ways, perhaps there is a shared lesson to be learned from the Hasidic sensitivity to the sacred process inherent in traditional Jewish practice.

FEAR, LOVE, AND TORAH STUDY

One of the major criticisms voiced by the early Hasidim against their opponents was the tendency in some circles to treat Torah study as an opportunity for intellectual debate *(pilpul)*, and not as a spiritual undertaking. In the next several texts, the early masters attempt to outline an alternative ethic for Torah study.

Fear, Love, and Torah Study

Be very careful not to waste time that could be spent
studying Torah....

As it is written,
"This book of Torah should not depart from your
mouth" (Joshua 1:8).

However, your learning must be for its own sake—
suffused with fear and love of God.
For Torah study without fear and love leads to
"God heard, and became angry" (Numbers 11:1) ...

Be very careful about learning for ulterior motives,
lest you turn your Torah into poison (Yoma 72b) ...

R. Menahem Mendel of Vitebsk, Likkutei Amarim, #2

This text is one of the classic statements about the tension between Torah study and *deveikut* in early Hasidism. Are these experiences mutually exclusive? Does one follow the other? Or can they occur simultaneously? If *deveikut* is the ultimate Hasidic goal, does this diminish the importance of Torah study?

Refining the Soul

When you study Torah
pause occasionally to cleave to God.

You must devote yourself to study, however,
even though you cannot cleave to God while doing so,
because Torah refines the soul:
"It is a tree of life to those who hold fast to it"
   (Proverbs 3:18) ...

R. Dov Baer of Mezeritch, Hayim V'Hesed, #2

R. Zev Wolf of Zhitomir (d. 1800), one of the leading students of the Great Maggid, describes his master's attempts to cleave to God when teaching Torah:

Once I heard the Maggid, of blessed memory, state explicitly: "I will teach you the best way to say words of Torah, which is as follows. Do not be aware of yourself, be as an ear listening to the way in which the "World of Speech" [the Shekhinah] speaks from within you.... As soon as you hear your own words, stop!" On many occasions I saw him [the Maggid] with my own eyes, as he opened his mouth to speak the words of Torah; he appeared to everyone around him as if he were not in this world at all, but as if the Shekhinah were speaking from his throat. (Or Ha-Meir, Ashdod, 1994, p. 213)

This teaching is obviously much more extreme than our *hanhagah*. In this case, not only does the Great Maggid demand that a person turn his attention away from his study partners, but he must completely abandon his own sense of self and allow the Divine to speak through him. There is a similar story told about the great sixteenth-century Jewish legal writer and mystic R. Joseph Karo (1488–1575). See Louis Jacobs, *The Jewish Mystics*, pp. 122–151.

A Divine Study Partner

Before uttering words of Torah,
bind yourself in your thoughts to the blessed Creator.

Imagine that you are speaking only to God,
with the aim of bringing Him pleasure,
without concern for anyone else's opinion.

Before speaking, say to yourself,
"I am not uttering these words of Torah to impress
    my companions,
because their approval and praise are not what I
    seek."

R. Dov Baer of Mezeritch, Hayim V'Hesed, #8

R. Zaddok ha-Kohen of Lublin (1823–1900), one of the foremost Torah scholars and Hasidic masters of his generation, speaks about the guidance of Torah in a similar manner, stressing the importance of connecting to the Divine light within the Torah:

> The term *torah* literally means "teaching," for the Torah indeed serves as a teacher and guide. This does not necessarily refer to the educational value of its statutes and laws, for even if one studies the order of Kodashim [the fifth order of the Talmud dealing mainly with animal sacrifices, and thus not obviously relevant to contemporary Jewish life], he is considered engaged in Torah study. But the guiding strength of Torah is its light, as our rabbis said in the *Midrash* [rabbinic legends and commentaries] on Lamentations (*Lamentations Rabbah*, proem 3): "The Torah's luminary power will cause their return to the good."
>
> The light of the Torah, which saves and protects, has its effect only on those who use it in the right way, that is, they engage in its study for its own sake [to bathe in its Divine light, and not for personal gain]. Then it is an elixir of life; for life and light are one and the same, as it says: "For with You is the fountain of life; in Your light do we see light" (Psalms 36:10).... (*Zidkat Ha-Zaddik, B'nei Brak: 1973–1974, p. 59*)

This translation is based on Norman Lamm, *The Religious Thought of Hasidism: Text and Commentary* (New York: Yeshiva University Press, 1999), pp. 232–233.

The Guidance of Torah

There will be times when something will come
　　your way
and you will be uncertain whether or not
　　to pursue it.

If you have studied Torah that day, however,
you will be able to determine your course of action
from your learning.

For this to occur,
you must sustain your connection to God.
Then, He will enable you to understand the
　　connection
between your studies and your life.

Tzava'at HaRivash, #31

CREATING ANGELS

Like other ancient religious traditions, Judaism has its share of angels. Whether depicted in mythical terms as winged creatures or in more abstract terms as impersonal cosmic forces, the *malakhim* ("angels," *malakh,* singular) occupy an important place in the Jewish imagination. In most cases, the angels are viewed as messengers of God, whose sole purpose it is to fulfill God's commands. Unlike human beings, the angels possess no independent will or desire. This applies both to angels of blessing and angels of judgment. In our text, it is we who "create" angels through our deeds. These angels serve as our advocates in reporting our accomplishments to God. For more on the relationship between the angels and human beings, see the note on the text "God Loves the Body," p. 110.

Creating Angels

Do not allow a single day to pass without performing
   a mitzvah,
whether great or small.

As our sages said,
"Be as *zahir* [careful] with a minor mitzvah as with a
   major one" (*Pirkei Avot* 2:1).

The word *zahir* is related to the expression,
"They who are wise *yaz'hiru* [will shine]"
   (Daniel 12:3).
Your soul will shine from a minor mitzvah just as it
   does from a major one,
for "The Merciful One desires the heart"
(*Sanhedrin* 106b).

This realization is of great importance,
for then you know that you have achieved something
   that day:
you have created an angel through your deeds,
as in the verse,
"If there be for him but one angel, among thousands,
   to declare his uprightness,
God shall have mercy on him"
(Job 33:23–24).

Tzava'at HaRivash, #17

The instruction to limit our feelings of sadness and regret is found throughout the Hasidic tradition. Beginning with the Ba'al Shem Tov, the Hasidic masters insist that excessive guilt and sadness deplete our spiritual energy and have far greater negative consequences than do minor imperfections in our religious lives. Frequently, the Rebbes describe the impulse toward guilt as the work of the "evil inclination"—the force within (and/or beyond) the human soul that seeks to sabotage or undermine our positive efforts.

> Sometimes the evil inclination tries to lead us astray by telling us that something we have done is a grave sin, when it is really just a minor infraction or perhaps no sin at all. It [the evil inclination] does this in order to make us sorrowful, for sorrow prevents us from carrying out our task of worshiping the Creator (*Tzava'at HaRivash*, #12).

The Joy of Service

Always be joyous,
for sadness is a great obstacle to serving God.

Even if you sin, heaven forbid,
do not let it stop you from serving God.

Limit your feelings of sadness and regret
to the particular transgression you have committed,
and then return to rejoice in the blessed Creator.

After all, you have repented
and you have no intention of returning to this
     foolishness again.

And even if you know that you are not fulfilling
every aspect of a particular mitzvah [commandment],
do not let this upset you;
rather, think of the blessed Creator
—He who judges hearts and intentions—
for He knows that you want to serve Him in the best
     possible way,
but that you cannot do so at this moment.

Strengthen yourself in the Creator,
for Scripture states:
"It is time to act for the Lord; [even if] they have
     violated Your teaching" (Psalms 119:126).

And when you perform an incomplete mitzvah,
pay no attention to the evil inclination
that wants to stop you from carrying out this deed.
Rather, say to it,
"In performing this mitzvah it is not my intention to
   anger God,
nor am I carrying it out for my own honor."

R. Dov Baer of Mezeritch, Hayim V'Hesed, *#3*

The Cosmic *Tzaddik* is the kabbalistic symbol for the male aspect of the Divine. As mentioned briefly in the note on "Arrogance Begets Anger" (p. 74), one of the central goals of the mystics is to unite the male and female (Shekhinah, or *Tzedek* in this text) aspects of the Divine through our actions in the lower world.

Tzedakah: The Root of Life

Tzedakah is the root of life.
When you give to others,
you raise the sparks from their broken state,
and you elevate your own soul.

The word *tzedakah* [charity] contains within it
the word *tzedek* [righteousness].

In acting as a *tzaddik* [righteous person],
you become a holy spark of the Cosmic *Tzaddik*
and you help elevate *Tzedek* from poverty and exile.

Enough said.

Here is the idea:

By carrying out a holy deed or an act of life-sustaining
    charity,
you redeem a spark from the evil forces,
and thus increase your own holiness....

> *R. Menahem Nahum of Chernobyl*, Hanhagot Yesharot

The term *et ratzon,* "a moment of heightened Divine favor" or "grace," is found in the book of Psalms 69:14, "As for me, may my prayer to You, YHVH, be an *et ratzon;* O God, in Your abundant kindness, answer me with the truth of Your salvation." This verse serves as the introduction to the Torah service on Sabbath afternoons and on the morning of major holidays, times that are considered particularly auspicious for prayer.

When Storm Clouds Gather

If at times you notice some negligence in your worship
   of the Creator,
it is all the more reason to rise with passion to serve
   Him.

This is certainly a moment of heightened Divine favor,
   as it is stated,
"Storm clouds surround Him,
righteousness and justice are the base of His throne!"
   (Psalms 97:2).

R. Hayim Heikel of Amdur, Hayim V'Hesed, #7

This text reflects the kabbalistic belief that through the proper fulfillment of the commandments one creates channels *(tzinorot)* for Divine blessing to flow through the world. On the influence of human action on the Divine in Jewish mysticism, see the notes to "Many Paths to God," p. 48, and "Arrogance Begets Anger," p. 74.

Mindful Practice

When performing a mitzvah
stop from time to time
and cleave to the blessed Creator.
Then you can perform your deed with greater joy.

When you understand the inner dimension of each
commandment
—how this mitzvah causes divinity to flow through all
the worlds—
it will help you to serve God with greater devotion.

R. Dov Baer of Mezeritch, Hayim V'Hesed, #10

Throughout the rabbinic tradition, there is a complicated relationship imagined between the angels and human beings (sometimes loving, sometimes competitive). Below is one well-known rabbinic legend illustrating some of the issues raised in our text (*Shabbat* 88b, translation based on Nahum N. Glatzer, *Hammer on the Rock: A Midrash Reader* [New York: Schocken Books, 1962], pp. 43–44):

> Rabbi Joshua ben Levi said: When Moses ascended to heaven, the ministering angels said to the Holy Blessed One: What is a man born of woman doing here? God said to them: He has come to receive the Torah. They said to Him: Is it the precious hidden treasure that first You hid 974 generations before the world was created that You seek to give to flesh and blood? What is man, that You are so interested in him? The Holy Blessed One then said to Moses: Reply to them ... Moses said to Him: Master of the universe, what is written in this Torah which you are about to give me? God answered, "I am the Lord your God who brought you out of the land of Egypt" (Exodus 20:2). Moses said to the angels: Did you go down to Egypt? Were you enslaved to Pharoah? Then what is the Torah to you? What else is written in it? "You shall have no other gods" (Exodus 20:3): Are you surrounded by nations that worship other gods? What else is written in it?..."Honor your father and mother" (Exodus 20:12): Do you have fathers and mothers? What else is written in it? "You
>
> *(continued)*

God Loves the Body

Why did God send the soul into the body?
He did so because of the body's lowly nature;
God derives great pleasure from it.

The soul is housed in a filthy vessel made of dust ...
and yet, it constantly gives praise and thanksgiving to
    the Holy Blessed One.

This is a major innovation.
In fact, God derives greater pleasure from human worship
than He does from the service and praises of the
    angels—
After all, He expects it from the angels....

Therefore, have faith that in performing a mitzvah
    with your body
—be it Torah study, prayer, or the rest of the
    commandments—
you arouse great pleasure in the Upper Worlds,
causing the Holy Blessed One and the Shekhinah, joy
    and satisfaction.

This should be your intention when performing any
    mitzvah....

Remember:
you can only bring pleasure to the Upper Worlds
by first arousing passion below,
that is, by experiencing your own physical pleasure.

R. Dov Baer of Mezeritch, Hayim V'Hesed, *#13–14*

shall not murder. You shall not commit adultery. You shall not steal"(Exodus 20:13): Is there any jealousy in your midst? Is there any will to do evil in your midst? At once they conceded to the Holy Blessed One. As it is written: "O Lord, Our Lord, How glorious is Your name in all the earth" (Psalms 8:2).

Part VI
In Speech & In Silence

Judaism has earned a reputation as a religion of words and deeds. Silent meditation is a practice we associate more readily with various Eastern traditions. Our daily experience strengthens this impression. How much silence was there in the last Jewish prayer service you attended? Our *tefilot* (prayers) tend to be overwhelmingly "wordy"; the *siddur* (prayer book) demonstrates the cumulative effect of generations of liturgists adding more and more words to our prayers.

The practice of silence emphasized by the Hasidic masters in this section may come as a blessing for those who have learned its benefits from other traditions, and who now wish to integrate it into their Jewish lives.

Yet the Hasidic masters were careful to point out that silent meditation is not an end in itself. It is a practice whose test must come in the world of action and interaction. The *hanhagot* provide us with guidance for meditation and prayer, but the ultimate challenge they pose is this: Can we maintain our spiritual focus in the world beyond the synagogue, study hall, or retreat center? Each night, as we review the events of the day, we must ask ourselves: Have I lived this day with awareness?

Enough said!

Choose Silence, Not Torah

"He who speaks too much brings sin"
(*Pirkei Avot* 1:5).
The meaning of this teaching is as follows:
the word sin *[het]* means deficiency *[hisaron]*.

Even when you speak with others about the wisdom
of the Torah,
silence is still preferable.

Silent contemplation offers greater possibilities for
connection with the Divine
than does discussion or speech.

R. Dov Baer of Mezeritch, Hayim V'Hesed, #9

This text expresses the Hasidic belief that the Divine-human relationship is reciprocal in nature. This is articulated in the kabbalistic expressions "arousal from above" *(itaruta di-le'eilah)* and "arousal from below" *(itaruta di-le'tatah)*. The first reflects God's desire to shower blessings upon creation and thus awaken us to the Divine presence. The second expresses the human desire to respond to the gifts of life by "arousing" the Divine through our positive actions. It is this arousal that causes God to pour forth more bounty (described here as vitality, *hiyut*) into the world. The Hasidic masters teach that it is the task of the mystic to maintain this cycle, ensuring that the Divine *shefa* (bounty) flows freely between heaven and earth.

The Cycle of Speech

Speech is the life force within you,
and this vitality comes from God.

Thus, when you speak "good speech,"
your words ascend on high and stir the Supernal
    Speech.

This, in turn,
causes further vitality to flow downward to you.

If, however, you say something negative,
the life force will depart from you and will not
    ascend,
leaving you severely weakened.

This is indicated in the Yiddish expression:
"*Er hot oysgeredt*—He has spoken it [the vitality]
    out!"

Tzava'at HaRivash, #103

The visualization of the sacred four-lettered name of God has been an important meditation technique in Jewish tradition for centuries. In fact, there is a widespread custom of placing *Shiviti* placards or wall hangings in synagogues or private homes for use during prayer and meditation. These signs usually include the Tetragrammaton at the center with the words, "I set *(Shiviti)* YHVH before me at all times" (Psalms 16:8), surrounding it in artistic fashion. For an example of this sacred art form, see the prayer book *Kol Haneshamah: Shabbat Vehagim* (Elkins Park, Pa.: The Reconstructionist Press, 2000) p. 89. Our *hanhagah* stresses the importance of cultivating this awareness not only in prayer or silent meditation, but in everyday life.

In its original context, the line from *Pirkei Avot* 4:19 deals with the teaching abilities of older and younger instructors. In urging the reader not to judge a person by his or her age the text states, "Do not look at the flask, but at its contents. You can find a new flask with old wine and an old flask which does not hold even new wine." This concept is broadened in our text to apply to one's vision of the world at large.

Mystical Engagement

"Silence shields wisdom" (*Pirkei Avot* 3:17).

It is easiest to attach yourself to the World of Thought
through silent meditation.

But if you are wise,
capable of maintaining your Divine focus at all times,
you can reach the same goal through your actions.

You can partake of all kinds of tasty foods and other
    delights,
without being distracted by these physical pleasures,
so that feasting and fasting are one and the same in
    your eyes.

You can look wherever you wish without losing your
    focus,
seeing the "four-lettered name" [YHVH] in all that
    you look at.

This follows the secret meaning of the verse
"I set YHVH before me at all times" (Psalms 16:8).

Similarly, our Rabbis taught:
"Do not look at the container, but what is in it"
    (*Pirkei Avot* 4:19).
The essence of the world is the Divine spirit within it ...

R. Dov Baer of Mezeritch, Hayim V'Hesed, #24

This text is part of a larger tradition that links human thoughts and emotions to the *sefirot*. The mystics believed that all human experience is rooted in the Divine, and therefore all of one's thoughts and feelings can be traced back to specific regions within the Godhead.

Emotional Mindfulness

Always be mindful of your thoughts and feelings.

If you experience a loving moment,
connect it to your love for the Creator.

If you have a hateful or angry moment,
connect it to your awe of God.

If you feel arrogant,
sit and study, for the Torah is God's pride ...

The basic principle is that you should not do anything
—great or small—
without first thinking about its Divine source....

R. Hayim Heikel of Amdur, Hayim V'Hesed, #2

The following is a reflection on the importance of solitude by one of Hasidism's most original thinkers, R. Nachman of Breslov (1772–1811):

> To be in solitude is a supreme advantage and the most important ideal. This means that one should set aside at least an hour or more during which he is alone in a room or in the field so that he can converse with the Maker in secret.... This prayer should be in the vernacular, namely, in these lands German [i.e., Yiddish]. For it is difficult for a man to express himself adequately in the holy tongue [i.e., Hebrew], and his heart cannot be in it to the same extent, for we do not usually converse in Hebrew. (*Likkutei Moharan, Tinyana*, no. 25, Mohilev, 1811)

This translation is based on that of Louis Jacobs, *Hasidic Thought,* pp. 62–63.

Solitude in Community

When you want to seclude yourself for private
    meditation,
have a companion with you.

It is dangerous to carry out this practice alone.

Two people should be in the room;
each one communing with the blessed Creator.

There will be times when you are so completely
    connected to God
that you will even be able to enter into solitude
in a room full of people.

Tzava'at HaRivash, #63

Here is R. Nachman of Breslov on the need for joy in the spiritual life:

> The general rule is that a person must try with all his might to be joyful, for by nature a person is drawn toward melancholy and sadness because of the events that befall him, and all people are full of suffering. It is, therefore, essential that one force himself with all his strength to be joyful always and to use every means to make himself rejoice, even if he has to resort to silly things. It is true that it is also very good for man to have a broken heart, yet this should only be in a certain hour. He should set aside an hour each day to break open his heart and pour out his speech to God.... But for the rest of the day he should only be in a state of joy. For it is easier to be led into melancholy from the state of brokenheartedness than it is to stumble, God forbid, through joy so that one is led to frivolity. (*Likkutei Moharan, Tinyana*, no. 24)

For more on the importance of joy in Hasidic spirituality, see the note on "The Joy of Service," p. 100.

A Single Thought

Clear your mind
so that you are not thinking too many thoughts.

Your only thought should be:
"How do I serve God with joy?"

The word *be'simhah* [with joy] has the same letters as
mahshavah [thought].
Therefore, all thoughts that come your way should be
directed to serving God joyfully.

As it is written,
"Many are the thoughts in one's mind,
but only the thought [literally, "counsel"] of God will
endure"
(Proverbs 19:21).

R. Menahem Nahum of Chernobyl, Hanhagot Yesharot

One of the many roles that the Rebbe (Hasidic master) plays for his community is that of spiritual counselor. In fact, in some Hasidic communities (HaBaD-Lubavitch) there has developed a practice known as *yehidut* (from the word, *yihud,* "unification," or *yehidah,* the highest level of the soul), in which master and disciple meet privately (not unlike contemporary psychology) to discuss the inner life of the disciple. The following is a striking definition of a "true" Hasidic master: "When you can find someone who can remove your innards, cleanse them, and return them to you while you are still alive—that is a Rebbe (R. Yitzhak Isaac Kolev)."

For more on the role of the Hasidic master as counselor, see Zalman Meshullam Schachter-Shalomi, *Spiritual Intimacy: A Study of Counseling in Hasidism* (Northvale, N.J.: Jason Aronson, 1991).

One interesting feature of our text is that the Hasid is advised not only to rely on the support of the Rebbe, but to seek out the help of friends as well.

Spiritual "Talk Therapy"

Share all your negative thoughts and feeling
—those that oppose our holy Torah, and are brought
   forth by the evil inclination—
with a spiritual mentor or trusted friend....

Do not leave out anything from these conversations
because of your shame or embarrassment.

By speaking about such things, by bringing them into
   the open,
you will break the power of the evil inclination,
so that it will not rise up against you at other times.

You will also receive the good counsel of your friend,
which is itself a wondrous treasure, a pathway
   to God.

> *R. Elimelech of Lizensk,* Tzetel Hakatan, *#13*

The discussion of the seven primordial creations is found in *Midrash Tanhuma* (Buber, *Naso:* 19). They are (1) the Throne of Glory, (2) the Torah, (3) the Temple, (4) the Forefathers, (5) Israel, (6) the name of the Messiah, and (7) *Teshuvah*. Some sages include the Garden of Eden.

By listing *teshuvah* as one of the entities that preceded the creation of the world, the Rabbis are making an important point about life: it is inconceivable to think of human existence without *teshuvah*. That is to say, life involves mistakes, foibles, and transgressions. Therefore, we need the possibility of repentance woven into the fabric of the universe.

Nightly Teshuvah

Be among those people who take stock of themselves
each night before going to sleep.

Give a nightly account of your sins and repent for
them.

Know that even a thought of repentance *[teshuvah]*
will suffice.

For *teshuvah* was one of the seven things
that preceded the creation of the world.

It is beyond time.

Therefore a single thought of *teshuvah* can "sweeten"
all of your misdeeds....

R. *Menahem Nahum of Chernobyl,* Hanhagot Yesharot

Tikkun Hatzot is a series of prayers for the restoration of Jerusalem to be recited after midnight. The kabbalists of Safed instituted this service in the sixteenth century. While commended by several early Hasidic masters, this practice generally fell out of use in Hasidic circles. Some Jews of Near Eastern origin continue this tradition today. See Adin Steinzaltz, *A Guide to Jewish Prayer* (New York: Schocken, 2000), pp. 84–86.

Joining Day and Night

Rise up from your sleep at midnight,
for this is a time of heightened Divine favor.

Serve God in the midnight hour and perform the
   Midnight Vigil *[Tikkun Hatzot]*.

As you join the words of the vigil to your morning
   prayers,
you unite with the Divine.
And you can bring forth whatever it is you seek
   from God.

Midnight prayer and worship is a great thing,
for it brings peace above.
If it were not for this service,
"those who are joined together"
[the male and female aspects of the Divine]
would be separated.

> R. *Menahem Nahum of Chernobyl*, Hanhagot Yesharot

Your Inner Voice

Always imagine that a person is standing next to you
calling out in a loud and clear voice,
awakening you to fulfill all of the details of these
hanhagot.

In time, when you accustom yourself to this practice,
a great spiritual arousal will well up in your soul,
a fiery flame, a Divine torch.

> R. *Elimelech of Lizensk,* Tzetel Hakatan, #12

Appendices:
Neo-Hasidic Hanhagot

Hillel Zeitlin

Hillel Zeitlin (1871–1942) was raised in Korma, Belorussia, under the influence of Lubavitch Hasidism and the Mitnaggedim. After serving as an itinerant Jewish studies teacher, he turned away from religion and became a secular writer and journalist, focusing on modern philosophy and politics. Settling in Warsaw in 1906, Zeitlin made a gradual return to a life of Hasidic piety. However, he remained intensely involved in the modern world, attempting to translate the teachings of the early Hasidic masters into language that was attractive to the young assimilated Jews of Warsaw. His home became a meeting place for socialists, rabbis, occultists, and secular intellectuals. According to legend, Zeitlin went to his death in the Warsaw Ghetto wrapped in *tallit* (prayer shawl) and *tefilin* (phylacteries), carrying a copy of the *Zohar* in his arms. The following is a selection of *hanhagot* from Zeitlin's diary entries from 1917.[1]

I wrote myself the following *hanhagot*:

1. Keep your lips sealed like two grinding stones that cleave to each other (*Sha'arei Kedushah,* Rabbi Hayim Vital).

2. Guard yourself from anger.

3. Be humble before all people, even the most lowly of them.

4. Be humble in your own eyes—for in truth what are we? What is our life? (from the *Birkhot Hashahar,* Early Morning Blessings)

5. Always let the mind rule the heart (*Tanya,* Rabbi Shneor Zalman of Liadi).

6. Thoughts of sin are more dangerous than sin itself; all who enter into such thoughts are barred from entering the court of the Holy Blessed One.

7. Do not enter into negotiations with your temptations (R. Nachman of Breslov).

8. Do not think too many thoughts: Plant one thought in your heart—to do only the will of your Father in heaven (R. Menahem Nahum of Chernobyl).

9. Even things that are permissible should not be undertaken unless they bring pleasure to your Father in heaven. And in this crucible of testing, save yourself from evil. Remember: Desire turns prohibition into permission. Therefore, address your temptations positively: "While it may be permissible to do this or that, will I be doing God's will? If not, why should I do it?" (the Seer of Lublin).

10. A pearl (or a recurrent teaching) from Rabbi Meir:

Learn with all your heart and soul to know My [God's] ways, and do not budge from the doorways of My Torah. Guard My Torah in your heart, and let My fear be before your eyes. Keep your mouth from all sin, cleanse and purify yourself from all intrusion and iniquity, and I will be with you always" (Babylonian Talmud, *Berakhot* 17a).

On *Rosh Hodesh Shevat* I wrote a series of spiritual directives for myself. Now, I am writing an additional list:

1. Cleave to the attribute of mercy until the end. Forgive all those who curse you. Perhaps God will bear your sin?

2. "Justice, justice shall you pursue" (Deuteronomy 16:20)—justice for yourself, for your family, and for all creatures. Cleave to the celestial source of justice (the *sefirah* of Yesod).

3. Always be joyful (internal joy, that is, quiet and restrained, no outbursts, God forbid), because sadness leads to evil deeds and thoughts.

4. Create an established routine for the maintenance of your body, because confusion and inconsistency harm the body and the soul.

5. "Many harm the wicked; but he who trusts in God will be surrounded by mercy" (Psalms 32:10). Do not fear; trust in God. And if you have sinned, return. Do not tarry. Do not think that you will not be accepted in *teshuvah* (repentance) because you have committed too many sins.

There is nothing standing between you and *teshuvah*. It is always possible to stand beneath the Throne of Glory if you make a true return with a pure heart.

6. And you, man, have mercy on your soul, which exists eternally. Bring her wondrous pleasures, beyond that which the eye can see [Isaiah 64:3]. Do not channel your desires into sin, lest you be rejected from light and sent into darkness. Have mercy on yourself and be kind to your soul, do not darken its radiance with the vanities of pleasure.

7. The following teaching is most essential: Close your mouth (except from speaking holy things, words of science and wisdom, and essential study; otherwise, keep your conversation with friends and guests as brief as possible). Close your eyes (to everything except the splendor of holiness). Focus your thoughts (think only of what you are doing now; do not scatter your thoughts). Think only pure thoughts, good and joyful. Sanctify yourself entirely for heaven. Be both a servant and a child to God. Do not be like a servant who performs his duties only at appointed times. Always be a servant and a child of the Divine.

Arthur Green

Arthur Green is professor of Jewish thought at Brandeis University and dean of the Rabbinical School at Boston's Hebrew College. An accomplished scholar in the field of Jewish mysticism, Green is also an acclaimed theologian and a leading figure in contemporary Jewish life. The following is a list of *hanhagot* he published in his book *Ehyeh: A Kabbalah for Tomorrow* (Woodstock, Vt.: Jewish Lights Publishing, 2003).

A Simple Serious Judaism for Today

1. Know that all of life is holy; all exists within the One. There is no time or place in which God's presence cannot be found. Meditate on this each day. Think about it at home, while commuting, at work, and back at home.

2. Take responsibility for your own spiritual life. It is

we who lock God out of our lives. Therefore open your heart, train your heart to fill up with God's presence and God's love. Be aware in each moment, no matter where you are or what you are doing, of the Divine radiance within you and all about you.

3. Train yourself to see the miracle of each day's arrival and departure. Celebrate the two sacred times of day, dawn and dusk, with prayer.

4. If your life is too complicated or too fast-paced to remain aware, work to live more simply and more slowly. Keep Shabbat as a time to slow down, live in harmony with nature, and reflect. Make room for Shabbat consciousness to enter your weekday world as well. Slow down.

5. Live the rhythm of the sacred calendar—Shabbat, holidays, seasons—as rich with traditional forms or as simply as your spirit desires. Remember that it is you who has to fill those forms with God's presence. It is the joy of your spirit that brings them to life!

6. Study Torah every day. Choose those texts, methods of learning, classes, and study partners that make for challenging and exciting learning experiences. If learning Torah is dull, you are doing something wrong. If it is exciting to you, teach others.

7. Share with others the fullness of spirit that flows from your religious life. Give to others beyond measure, just as no one has measured the great gifts you receive. Give of yourself: give time, not just money; give directly, not just impersonally. Above all, give love.

8. Live in community with those who most closely share your path, but live in genuine openness to learning from others who do not. In choosing your life partner and friends, try to find those who will be open to and encourage your quest. Make space for spiritual awareness in your

marriage or partnership. Talk about the holiness of your love, seeing it as a part of your love of God.

9. Recognize every person as the image of God. Work to see the Divine image especially in those who themselves seem oblivious to it. Seek out divinity in those who annoy, anger, or frustrate you. Hope to find and uplift sparks of holy light, even where it seems hardest. Do all the work that is needed to help others to discover the image of God within themselves.

10. Learn to recognize evil, usually a creation of frightened, selfish, or otherwise distorted human hearts. Always try to transform it, but be ready to confront it and to battle it with courage when there is no other choice.

11. Love the Jewish people, the root from which you are drawn. Work to improve the quality of Jewish life, both in Israel, where Judaism is most fully lived and tested in our day, and wherever you are. Contribute to the growth of Jewish life spiritually, intellectually, culturally, emotionally, in whatever way you can. Be part of the great healing process within the Jewish people, the repair of feelings and attitudes created by centuries of persecution and by the terrible Holocaust of the past century, a healing that is not yet completed.

12. Work toward the expansion of the sacred into new realms, the creation of new religious forms appropriate to our age. Treat Judaism as a growing, dynamic tradition, one that wants to creatively engage the future as much as it wants to preserve the legacy of the past.

13. Share the witness of God's oneness with all who want to receive it. Witness by public prayer, by teaching, but mostly by doing. Be willing to share in mutual witness with those of other faith paths. Open your heart to be inspired by them, without losing confidence in the path that is your own.

14. Recognize once again that all of existence is Divine. Devote yourself to the healthy preservation of life: your own, that of people around you, but also of all creatures on our much-threatened planet. Engage in the great collective mitzvah of our time—that of protecting this earth and its resources for generations that will come after us. Come to see humanity as part of the great chorus of all creatures, each one an embodiment of divinity and a vital singer in life's great, complex, painful, but ultimately joyous and triumphant song: Halleluyah!

Notes

Introduction

1. The Hebrew word *Hasid,* from which the term "Hasidism" stems, is best translated as "pious one." It is a term applied to a number of different individuals and groups throughout Jewish history, including various rabbinic sages and medieval mystics. In its Eastern European context, to be a Hasid meant that one was the disciple of a particular spiritual master (Rebbe or *tzaddik*).

2. The name Ba'al Shem Tov (or Ba'al Shem, "Master of the Name") was a common title given to Jewish folk healers at the time. A person was designated as a "Master of the Good Name" if he possessed the ability to use various Divine names (the "Good Name" refers to God, not to the person) in the creation of amulets and other magical healing devices. Israel ben Eliezer emerged as the most important Ba'al Shem and is, therefore, often referred to by this title.

3. There has been a great deal of speculation about the life of the Ba'al Shem Tov. Like other influential religious figures, he is the subject of countless legends retold by generations of adoring Hasidic faithful. The most important collection of legends about the Ba'al Shem Tov is *Shivhei HaBesht* (1814), translated into English by Dan Ben-Amos and Jerome M. Mintz as *In Praise of the Ba'al Shem Tov* (Northvale, N.J.: Jason Aronson, 1993). More recently, scholars have begun to investigate the life of Israel ben Eliezer, attempting to tease apart the man from the legends. Two such attempts are *Founder of Hasidism: The Search for the Historical Ba'al Shem Tov,* by Moshe Rosman (Berkeley: University of California Press, 1996), and

145

Ba'al Ha-Shem: The Besht—Magic, Mysticism, Leadership (Hebrew), by Immanuel Etkes (Jerusalem: Magnes Press, 2000).

4. The word *kabbalah,* literally "that which has been received," or "the receiving," is the Hebrew term commonly used to describe the Jewish mystical tradition as a whole. It is also the technical term for the period of intense Jewish mystical flowering in southern France and northern Spain in the thirteenth and fourteenth centuries (sometimes referred to as the period of "classical Kabbalah"). Here we refer to the entirety of the Jewish mystical tradition prior to the rise of Eastern European Hasidism. As revivalists, the Hasidim carefully selected from the vast treasure trove of Kabbalah (and other Jewish traditions) in fashioning their unique program for Jewish life. For a scholarly introduction to the classical Kabbalah, see Elliot K. Ginsberg, *The Sabbath in the Classical Kabbalah* (Albany: State University of New York Press, 1989), pp. 1–58. For an introduction to the Jewish mystical tradition as a whole, see Lawrence Kushner's *The Way into Jewish Mysticism* (Woodstock, Vt.: Jewish Lights, 2002).

5. The following is a well-known legend about the "conversion" experience of the Great Maggid to Hasidism. The tale conveys the Hasidic belief in the Ba'al Shem Tov's supernatural powers and his skill as a master pedagogue. This version of the legend is based on that found in Louis Jacobs's *Hasidic Thought* (New York: Behrman House, 1976), pp. 3–4.

I heard a certain Hasid tell the story of what happened when Rabbi Dov Baer of Mezeritch, of blessed memory, heard word of the fame of the holy Rabbi, the Ba'al Shem Tov. Rabbi Dov Baer heard that people were flocking to the Besht and how he accomplished awesome and tremendous feats by the power of his prayers. Now Rabbi Dov Baer was a most rigorous scholar, thoroughly familiar with the whole of the Talmud and all of the [Jewish legal] Codes, and he possessed ten measures of knowledge in the science of the Kabbalah. Astonished by the reports he had heard concerning the high rank of the Ba'al Shem Tov, Rabbi Dov Baer decided that he would journey to meet the Besht to put him to the test....When he eventually came to the home of the Ba'al Shem Tov, Rabbi Dov Baer thought that he would hear words of Torah, but instead the Besht told him a tale of how he had recently undertaken a journey....When Rabbi Dov Baer returned the next day, the Ba'al Shem Tov continued telling tales. Now all of these tales contained great and marvelous wisdom if one could only understand them. But since Rabbi Dov Baer failed to appreciate this he returned to his inn, saying to his servant: "I wish to return home immediately, but since it is so dark out right now we will wait to travel until the moon shines brightly in the night sky." At midnight, just as Rabbi Dov Baer was preparing to leave, the Ba'al Shem Tov sent his servant to summon him; Dov Baer heeded the summons. The Ba'al Shem Tov asked him, "Are you a scholar?' and he answered "Yes." "So have I heard," said the Ba'al Shem Tov. "And do you know the science of the Kabbalah?" "Yes I do," said Dov Baer. The Besht then instructed his servant to bring a copy of the mystical text *Etz Hayim,* and the Besht showed Dov Baer a passage in the book. Rabbi Dov Baer looked at the passage and began to expound upon it. But the Besht said, "You have not the slightest idea of the meaning of this passage." So Dov Baer looked at it again. "I am certain that I have explained this text correctly," he said, "but if your honor knows of another meaning, let him tell it to me and I will judge which is better." Upon which the Besht said, "Arise!" and he rose to his feet. Now this text made mention of the names of several angels, and no sooner did the

Besht begin reciting these names than the whole house filled up with light, fire burning all around it, and the angels actually appeared. The Besht then said to Rabbi Dov Baer, "It is true that your explanation of the text was correct, however your explanation had no soul in it." At that moment, Dov Baer ordered his servant to journey home while he, himself, stayed on in the home of the Ba'al Shem Tov, from whom he learned great and deep sources of wisdom. The Hasid heard all of this from Rabbi Dov Baer's own holy mouth.

6. For a discussion of the relationship of the Maggid to his circle of associates, see Simon Dubnow's article "The Maggid of Miedzyrzecz [Polish spelling], His Associates, and the Center in Volhynia," reprinted in *Essential Papers on Hasidism,* edited by Gershon D. Hundert (New York: New York University Press, 1991), pp. 58–85; and Ada Rapoport-Albert, "Hasidism After 1772: Structural Continuity and Change," *Hasidism Reappraised* (London: Littman Library of Jewish Civilization, 1997), pp. 76–140.

7. On the fierce conflicts between the Hasidim and the Mitnaggedim, see Mordecai L. Wilensky, "Hasidic-Mitnaggedic Polemics in the Jewish Communities of Eastern Europe: The Hostile Phase," reprinted in *Essential Papers on Hasidism,* pp. 244–271; and, more recently, Allan Nadler, *The Faith of the Mithnagdim* (Baltimore: Johns Hopkins University Press, 1997), especially pp. 11–28 and 151–170.

8. Arthur Green has sketched a helpful timeline of the four major phases of Hasidism:

1750–1815—The period of Challenge and Growth

1815–1880—The period of Control and Struggle with *Haskalah* (Jewish Enlightenment)

1880–1945—The period of Decline and Destruction

1945–present—The period of Rebirth and Transplantation

See Green's *The Language of Truth: The Torah Commentary of the Sefat Emet* (Philadelphia: Jewish Publication Society, 1998), p. xlix.

9. For an interesting sociological treatment of the spiritualization of North American religion in the second half of the twentieth century, see Robert Wuthnow's *After Heaven: Spirituality in America Since the 1950s* (Berkeley: University of California Press, 2001).

10. Buber's most important collection of Hasidic tales—themselves now classics in Western spiritual literature—is the two-volume work *Tales of the Hasidim (Early and Later Masters)*, edited and translated by Olga Marx (New York: Schocken Books, 1947–1948). For insight into Buber's approach to Hasidism, see the essays in his *Hasidism and Modern Man*, edited and translated by Maurice Friedman (New York: Horizon Press, 1958); and Part II of *The Martin Buber Reader: Essential Writings,* edited by Asher D. Biemann (New York: Palgrave Macmillan, 2002).

11. For an introduction to Scholem's approach to Hasidism, see "Hasidism: The Latest Phase," in his classic study of the Jewish mystical tradition, *Major Trends in Jewish Mysticism* (New York: Schocken Books, 1995), pp. 325–350.

12. The debate between Buber and Scholem on the "correct" reading of Hasidic materials is itself the subject of much scholarly discussion. See, for example, Moshe Idel's treatment of this issue in the introduction to his book *Hasidism: Between Ecstasy and Magic* (Albany: State University of New York Press, 1995), especially pp. 2–8.

13. One important exception to this statement is the fine work by the Israeli scholar Zev Gries. His book *The Hanhagot Literature: Its History and Place in the Life of the Beshtian Hasidim* [Hebrew] (Jerusalem: Bialik, 1989) has been a most helpful resource in the preparation of this volume. Arthur Green has translated two brief lists of *hanhagot* by R.

Menahem Nahum of Chernobyl; see *Menahem Nahum of Chernobyl: Upright Practices, The Light of Eyes* (Ramsey, N.J.: Paulist Press, 1982), pp. 31–42. Louis Jacobs has translated a small number of the *hanhagot* of various masters; see his *Hasidic Thought,* pp. 78–81, 103–107, and 147–148. Jacob Immanuel Schochet has translated the classic Hasidic work *Tzava'at HaRivash (1792–1793),* which contains an assortment of early Hasidic teachings, including many *hanhagot.* See *Tzava'at HaRivash: The Testament of the Baal Shem Tov* (Brooklyn: Kehot Publication Society, 1998). While we have benefited from the outstanding work of these scholars, our translations differ in many cases.

14. Moses Cordovero (1522–1570), spiritual leader of the mystical circle of Safed, was the disciple of Joseph Karo, author of the great legal work the *Shulkhan Arukh* (and a mystic himself), and the kabbalistic poet Shlomo Alkabetz (also Cordovero's brother-in-law), writer of the popular Friday evening prayer *Lekha Dodi.* Cordovero was the author of several important mystical works, including extensive treatises on theology and ethics. For more information on Moses Cordovero, see Joseph Ben-Shlomo's entry in Gershom Scholem's *Kabbalah* (New York: Quadrangle/New York Times Books, 1974), pp. 401–404.

Isaac Luria (1534–1572), commonly referred to as the holy Ari, "Lion" (from the initials of his title and name), is perhaps the single most original thinker in the history of the Kabbalah. Born and raised in Egypt, Luria spent only a few years in Safed, before dying in an epidemic at the age of thirty-eight. Nonetheless, he was recognized as an extraordinary thinker and a saintly personality and gathered around himself a number of impressive disciples in a short period of time. After his death, Luria's fame grew as a person possessed of the "holy spirit," and he became a legend throughout the Jewish world. Although he did not record his own teachings, several of his students, Hayim Vital being the most prolific among them, slowly disseminated his ideas. Luria built upon the teachings of the great medieval mystical work the *Zohar*, creating a richly mythical and highly complex theological system. For more on Luria, see Lawrence Fine's study *Isaac Luria: Doctor of the Soul, Healer of the Cosmos* (Stanford, Calif.: Stanford University Press, 2003).

15. See Lawrence Fine, *Safed Spirituality* (Ramsey, N.J.: Paulist Press, 1984).

16. While it is absolutely crucial to study the difficult and disturbing texts of the Hasidic tradition, given the aims of this book we felt that this was not the appropriate place to delve into this matter. For a preliminary discussion of this issue, see Or N. Rose's article "The Image of the Non-Jew in Early Hasidism: A Theological Critique," forthcoming in the published proceedings from Awakening, Yearning, and Renewal: A Conference on the Hasidic Roots of Contemporary Jewish Spiritual Expression, sponsored by the JCC in Manhattan, Bard College, and UJA-Federation of New York.

17. The British scholar Naftalie Lowenthal makes brief mention of these two types of *hanhagot* in his book *Communicating the Infinite: The Emergence of the Habad School* (Chicago: University of Chicago Press, 1990), p. 231.

18. See Arthur Green, "Teachings of the Hasidic Masters," in *Back to the Sources*, edited by Barry W. Holtz (New York: Schocken Books, 1984), pp. 361–401.

19. For a wonderful reflection on the art of translation, see Walter Benjamin's classic essay "The Task of the Translator," in *Illuminations: Essays and Reflections*, edited by Hannah Arendt and translated by Harry Zohn (New York: Schocken Books, 1968), pp. 69–82. On the specific challenges of translating Hasidic texts into English, see Arthur Green's article "On Translating Hasidic Homilies," *Prooftexts* 3, no. 1 (Winter 1983): pp. 63–72.

20. Here we follow in the footsteps of other contemporary trans-
lators of Jewish mystical texts, especially Daniel C. Matt, editor
of *The Essential Kabbalah* (San Francisco: HarperCollins,
1995) and *Zohar: Annotated & Explained* (Woodstock, Vt.:
SkyLight Paths Publishing, 2002); and Arthur Green and
Barry W. Holtz, editors of *Your Word Is Fire: The Hasidic
Masters on Contemplative Prayer* (Woodstock, Vt.: Jewish
Lights Publishing, 1993).
21. Brief biographies of Zeitlin and Green accompany their *hanhagot* (see pp. 137, 141).
22. See Buber, *Tales of the Hasidim: Early Masters*, p. 107.

Appendix: Hillel Zeitlin

1. Our translation is based on that of Moshe Waldoks in his
unpublished doctoral dissertation, *Hillel Zeitlin: The Early
Years (1894–1919)* (Waltham, Mass.: Brandeis University,
1984), pp. 244–248.

Glossary

Aleinu   The closing hymn of all major Jewish prayer services.

Avodah be'gashmiut   Service through the physical.

derashah, derashot (plural)   Homily(ies), sermon (s).

deveikut   Awareness of God, "cleaving" to God, connection to God, unification with God.

gadlut   "Greatness," expanded consciousness, heightened awareness (opposite of *katnut*).

hesed   Loving-kindness.

het   Sin.

hisaron   Deficiency.

hitlahavut   Enthusiasm, ecstasy, rapture.

Hokhmah   "Wisdom," the first identifiable emanation of the Divine according to the Hasidic masters (the second *sefirah* in many kabbalistic works)

Kabbalah   The Jewish mystical tradition; the flowering of Jewish mysticism in southern France and northern Spain in the thirteenth and fourteenth centuries.

katnut   "Smallness," constricted consciousness, limited awareness.

kavannah   Inner focus, intention, direction.

kelipot   "Husks," "shards," forces of evil.

Maggid   Preacher.

mikveh Ritual bath.

minyan Prayer quorum of ten adults (ten men in Orthodox tradition).

Mitnagged "Opponents" of Hasidism.

mitzvah, mitzvot (plural) "Commandment(s)," Jewish ritual and/or ethical action(s).

Pirkei Avot Ethics of the Fathers, a popular ethical treatise from the early rabbinic period (first century C.E.).

Sefer Ha-Zohar *The Book of Splendor,* the most revered Jewish mystical text, first disseminated in Spain in the late thirteenth century by Moses ben Shem Tov de Leon.

sefirah, sefirot (plural) "Number(s)," the ten primal divine emanations.

Shekhinah Female indwelling presence of God, tenth *sefirah.*

siddur Prayer book.

simhah Joy.

sippur, sippurim (plural) Story(ies), tale(s).

tefilah Prayer.

teshuvah Repentance; return.

tikkun Repair, restoration.

Tikkun Hatzot Midnight Vigil, a kabbalistic ritual of prayer and study for the fallen Temple in Jerusalem, instituted by the sixteenth-century mystics of Safed.

tzaddik Righteous one, common term for the Hasidic master.

tzedakah Charity.

Tzinorot Channels through which divine blessing flows between heaven and earth.

Yetzer Ha'ra The Evil Inclination, the human urge to do evil.

YHVH The Tetragrammaton, the ineffable or unspeakable name of God.

zerizut Eagerness, enthusiasm.

zivug Coupling, human and Divine.

Bibliography of Hasidic Sources

Elimelech of Lizensk, *Noam Elimelech* [Lemberg, 1788], edited by G. Nigal (2 volumes; Jerusalem, 1978).

Hayim Heikel of Amdur, *Hayim V'Hesed* [Warsaw, 1891] (Jerusalem, 1975).

Menahem Mendel of Vitebsk, *Likkutei Amarim* (Lemberg, 1911).

Menahem Nahum of Chernobyl, *Meor Eynayim* [Slavita, 1798] (Jerusalem, 1966, including the *Hanhagot Yesharot*), published in English as *Menahem Nahum of Chernobyl: Upright Practices, The Light of the Eyes*, translated by Arthur Green (Ramsey, N.J.: Paulist Press, 1982).

Rothenberg, Hayim Shlomo, editor. *Hanhagot Tzaddikim* (Jerusalem: Sifrei Kodesh, 1988). 3 volumes.

Tzava'at HaRivash [Ostrog? 1793; Zolkiev, 1795], edited by J. I. Schochet (Brooklyn, N.Y.: Kehot Publishing, 1975), published in English as *Tzava'at HaRivash: The Testament of Rabbi Israel Baal Shem Tov*, translated by Jacob Imannuel Schochet (Brooklyn, N.Y.: Kehot Publishing, 1998).

Suggestions for Further Reading

*Readings that may be of special interest to the beginner.

*Ariel, David. *The Mystic Quest: An Introduction to Jewish Mysticism.* New York: Schocken Books, 1992.
*Breslov Research Institute. *The Empty Chair: Finding Hope and Joy—Timeless Wisdom from a Hasidic Master, Rebbe Nachman of Breslov.* Woodstock, Vt.: Jewish Lights Publishing, 1994.
*Breslov Research Institute. *The Gentle Weapon: Prayers for Everyday and Not-So-Everyday Moments—Timeless Wisdom from the Teachings of the Hasidic Master, Rebbe Nachman of Breslov.* Woodstock, Vt.: Jewish Lights Publishing, 1999.
Buber, Martin. *Hasidism and Modern Man.* Translated and edited by Maurice Friedman. Atlantic Highlands, N.J.: Humanities Press International, 1988.
*———. *Tales of the Hasidim.* New York: Schocken Books, 1947–1948.
Buxbaum, Yitzhak. *Jewish Spiritual Practices.* Northvale, N.J.: Jason Aronson, 1990.
Fine, Lawrence, ed. and trans. *Safed Spirituality: Rules of Mystical Piety, The Beginning of Wisdom.* Ramsey, N.J.: Paulist Press, 1985.
Ginsberg, Elliot. *The Sabbath in the Classical Kabbalah.* Albany: State University of New York Press, 1989.
*Green, Arthur. *Ehyeh: A Kabbalah for Tomorrow.* Woodstock, Vt.: Jewish Lights Publishing, 2003.
Green, Arthur, ed. and trans. *Menahem Nahum of Chernobyl: Upright Practices, The Light of the Eyes.* Ramsey, N.J.: Paulist Press, 1982.

Green, Arthur. *Tormented Master: The Life and Spiritual Quest of Rabbi Nahman of Bratslav.* Woodstock, Vt.: Jewish Lights Publishing, 1992.

*Green, Arthur, and Barry W. Holtz. *Your Word Is Fire: The Hasidic Masters on Contemplative Prayer.* 3rd ed. Woodstock, Vt.: Jewish Lights Publishing, 1993.

Heschel, Abraham Joshua. *The Circle of the Baal Shem Tov: Studies in Hasidism.* Edited by Samuel H. Dresner. Chicago: University of Chicago Press, 1985.

Hundert, Gershon, ed. *Essential Papers on Hasidism: Origins to Present.* New York: New York University Press, 1991.

Idel, Moshe. *Hasidism: Between Ecstasy and Magic.* Albany: State University of New York Press, 1995.

Jacobs, Louis. *Hasidic Prayer.* New York: Schocken Books, 1972.

*———. *Jewish Mystics.* London: Schocken Books, 1976.

*———. *Hasidic Thought.* New York: Behrman House, 1976.

*Jacobson, Yoram. *Hasidic Thought.* Translated by Jonathan Chipman. Tel Aviv: MOD Press, 1998.

*Kushner, Lawrence. *The Way into Jewish Mystical Tradition.* Woodstock, Vt.: Jewish Lights Publishing, 2001.

*Lamm, Norman. *The Religious Thought of Hasidism: Text and Commentary.* New York: Yeshiva University Press, 1999.

*Matt, Daniel C. *The Essential Kabbalah: The Heart of Jewish Mysticism.* San Francisco: HarperCollins, 1995.

Mykoff, Moshe. *Seventh Heaven: Celebrating Shabbat with Rebbe Nachman of Breslov.* Woodstock, Vt.: Jewish Lights Publishing, 2003.

Rappaport-Albert, Ada, ed. *Hasidism Reappraised.* London: Littman Library of Jewish Civilization, 1997.

Rosman, Moshe. *Founder of Hasidism: A Quest for the Historical Ba'al Shem Tov.* Berkeley: University of California Press, 1996.

Schatz Uffenheimer, Rivka. *Hasidism as Mysticism: Quietistic Elements in Eighteenth-Century Hasidic Thought.* Translated by Jonathan Chipman. Princeton, N.J.: Princeton University Press/Jerusalem: Magnes Press, Hebrew University of Jerusalem, 1993.

*Scholem, Gershom. *Major Trends in Jewish Mysticism.* 5th ed. New York: Schocken Books, 1995.

*Shapiro, Rami. *Hasidic Tales: Annotated & Explained.* Woodstock, Vt.: SkyLight Paths Publishing, 2004.

Weiss, Joseph. *Studies in East European Jewish Mysticism and Hasidism.* 2nd ed. Edited and translated by David Goldstein. London: Littman Library of Jewish Civilization, 1997.

*Wineman, Aryeh. *The Hasidic Parable: An Anthology with Commentary.* Philadelphia: Jewish Publication Society, 2001.

Acknowledgments

We wish to thank the following people for their assistance with this project:

Daniel Abrams
Avi Bernstein
Shai Held
Nehemiah Polen
The Leader-Almog family
The Rose family
Judith Rosenbaum
The members of the Synagogue at Malden Bridge
Stuart M. Matlins, publisher of Jewish Lights
Emily Wichland, managing editor, and
the entire Jewish Lights staff.

Bar/Bat Mitzvah

The Bar/Bat Mitzvah Memory Book
An Album for Treasuring the Spiritual Celebration
By Rabbi Jeffrey K. Salkin and Nina Salkin
A unique album for preserving the spiritual memories of the day, and for recording plans for the Jewish future ahead. Contents include space for creating or recording family history; teachings received from rabbi, cantor, and others; mitzvot and *tzedakot* chosen and carried out, etc.
8 x 10, 48 pp, Deluxe Hardcover, 2-color text, ribbon marker, ISBN 1-58023-111-X **$19.95**

Bar/Bat Mitzvah Basics: A Practical Family Guide to Coming of Age Together
Edited by Helen Leneman. Foreword by Rabbi Jeffrey K. Salkin.
6 x 9, 240 pp, Quality PB, ISBN 1-58023-151-9 **$18.95**

For Kids—Putting God on Your Guest List: How to Claim the Spiritual Meaning
of Your Bar or Bat Mitzvah *By Rabbi Jeffrey K. Salkin*
6 x 9, 144 pp, Quality PB, ISBN 1-58023-015-6 **$14.95** *For ages 11–12*

Putting God on the Guest List: How to Reclaim the Spiritual Meaning of Your
Child's Bar or Bat Mitzvah *By Rabbi Jeffrey K. Salkin*
6 x 9, 224 pp, Quality PB, ISBN 1-879045-59-1 **$16.95**

Tough Questions Jews Ask: A Young Adult's Guide to Building a Jewish Life
By Rabbi Edward Feinstein 6 x 9, 160 pp, Quality PB, ISBN 1-58023-139-X **$14.95** *For ages 13 & up*
Also Available: **Tough Questions Jews Ask Teacher's Guide**
8½ x 11, 72 pp, PB, ISBN 1-58023-187-2 **$8.95**

Bible Study/Midrash

Hineini in Our Lives: Learning How to Respond to Others through 14 Biblical Texts,
and Personal Stories *By Norman J. Cohen*
6 x 9, 240 pp, Hardcover, ISBN 1-58023-131-4 **$23.95**

Ancient Secrets: Using the Stories of the Bible to Improve Our Everyday Lives
By Rabbi Levi Meier, Ph.D. 5½ x 8½, 288 pp, Quality PB, ISBN 1-58023-064-4 **$16.95**

Moses—The Prince, the Prophet His Life, Legend & Message for Our Lives
By Rabbi Levi Meier, Ph.D.
6 x 9, 224 pp, Quality PB, ISBN 1-58023-069-5 **$16.95**; Hardcover, ISBN 1-58023-013-X **$23.95**

Self, Struggle & Change: Family Conflict Stories in Genesis and Their Healing Insights
for Our Lives *By Norman J. Cohen* 6 x 9, 224 pp, Quality PB, ISBN 1-879045-66-4 **$16.95**

Voices from Genesis: Guiding Us through the Stages of Life *By Norman J. Cohen*
6 x 9, 192 pp, Quality PB, ISBN 1-58023-118-7 **$16.95**

Congregation Resources

Becoming a Congregation of Learners: Learning as a Key to Revitalizing
Congregational Life *By Isa Aron, Ph.D. Foreword by Rabbi Lawrence A. Hoffman.*
6 x 9, 304 pp, Quality PB, ISBN 1-58023-089-X **$19.95**

Finding a Spiritual Home: How a New Generation of Jews Can Transform the
American Synagogue *By Rabbi Sidney Schwarz*
6 x 9, 352 pp, Quality PB, ISBN 1-58023-185-3 **$19.95**

Jewish Pastoral Care: A Practical Handbook from Traditional & Contemporary Sources
Edited by Rabbi Dayle A. Friedman 6 x 9, 464 pp, Hardcover, ISBN 1-58023-078-4 **$35.00**

The Self-Renewing Congregation: Organizational Strategies for Revitalizing
Congregational Life *By Isa Aron, Ph.D. Foreword by Dr. Ron Wolfson.*
6 x 9, 304 pp, Quality PB, ISBN 1-58023-166-7 **$19.95**

Or phone, fax, mail or e-mail to: **JEWISH LIGHTS Publishing**
Sunset Farm Offices, Route 4 • P.O. Box 237 • Woodstock, Vermont 05091
Tel: (802) 457-4000 • Fax: (802) 457-4004 • www.jewishlights.com
Credit card orders: **(800) 962-4544** (8:30AM–5:30PM ET Monday–Friday)
Generous discounts on quantity orders. SATISFACTION GUARANTEED. Prices subject to change.

Children's Books

Because Nothing Looks Like God
By Lawrence and Karen Kushner

What is God like? The first collaborative work by husband-and-wife team Lawrence and Karen Kushner introduces children to the possibilities of spiritual life. Real-life examples of happiness and sadness invite us to explore, together with our children, the questions we all have about God, no matter what our age.

11 x 8½, 32 pp, Full-color illus., Hardcover, ISBN 1-58023-092-X **$16.95** *For ages 4 & up*

Also Available: **Because Nothing Looks Like God Teacher's Guide**
8½ x 11, 22 pp, PB, ISBN 1-58023-140-3 **$6.95** *For ages 5–8*

Board Book Companions to *Because Nothing Looks Like God*
5 x 5, 24 pp, Full-color illus., SkyLight Paths Board Books, **$7.95** each *For ages 0–4*

What Does God Look Like? ISBN 1-893361-23-3
How Does God Make Things Happen? ISBN 1-893361-24-1
Where Is God? ISBN 1-893361-17-9

The 11th Commandment: Wisdom from Our Children
by The Children of America

"If there were an Eleventh Commandment, what would it be?" Children of many religious denominations across America answer this question—in their own drawings and words.

8 x 10, 48 pp, Full-color illus., Hardcover, ISBN 1-879045-46-X **$16.95** *For all ages*

Jerusalem of Gold: Jewish Stories of the Enchanted City
Retold by Howard Schwartz. Full-color illus. by Neil Waldman.

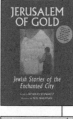

A beautiful and engaging collection of historical and legendary stories for children. Each celebrates the magical city that has served as a beacon for the Jewish imagination for three thousand years. Draws on Talmud, midrash, Jewish folklore, and mystical and Hasidic sources.

8 x 10, 64 pp, Full-color illus., Hardcover, ISBN 1-58023-149-7 **$18.95** *For ages 7 & up*

The Book of Miracles: A Young Person's Guide to Jewish Spiritual Awareness
By Lawrence Kushner. All-new illustrations by the author.

6 x 9, 96 pp, 2-color illus., Hardcover, ISBN 1-879045-78-8 **$16.95** *For ages 9–13*

In Our Image: God's First Creatures
By Nancy Sohn Swartz

9 x 12, 32 pp, Full-color illus., Hardcover, ISBN 1-879045-99-0 **$16.95** *For ages 4 & up*

From SKYLIGHT PATHS PUBLISHING

Becoming Me: A Story of Creation
By Martin Boroson. Full-color illus. by Christopher Gilvan-Cartwright.

Told in the personal "voice" of the Creator, a story about creation and relationship that is about each one of us. In simple words and with radiant illustrations, the Creator tells an intimate story about love, about friendship and playing, about our world—and about ourselves.

8 x 10, 32 pp, Full-color illus., Hardcover, ISBN 1-893361-11-X **$16.95** *For ages 4 & up*

Ten Amazing People: And How They Changed the World
By Maura D. Shaw. Foreword by Dr. Robert Coles. Full-color illus. by Stephen Marchesi.

Black Elk • Dorothy Day • Malcolm X • Mahatma Gandhi • Martin Luther King, Jr. • Mother Teresa • Janusz Korczak • Desmond Tutu • Thich Nhat Hanh • Albert Schweitzer • This vivid, inspirational, and authoritative book will open new possibilities for children by telling the stories of how ten of the past century's greatest leaders changed the world in important ways.

8½ x 11, 48 pp, Full-color illus., Hardcover, ISBN 1-893361-47-0 **$17.95** *For ages 7 & up*

Where Does God Live? *By August Gold and Matthew J. Perlman*
Using simple, everyday examples that children can relate to, this colorful book helps young readers develop a personal understanding of God.

10 x 8½, 32 pp, Full-color photo illus., Quality PB, ISBN 1-893361-39-X **$8.95** *For ages 3–6*

Children's Books
by Sandy Eisenberg Sasso

Adam & Eve's First Sunset: God's New Day
Engaging new story explores fear and hope, faith and gratitude in ways that will delight kids and adults—inspiring us to bless each of God's days and nights.
9 x 12, 32 pp, Full-color illus., Hardcover, ISBN 1-58023-177-2 **$17.95** *For ages 4 & up*

But God Remembered
Stories of Women from Creation to the Promised Land
Four different stories of women—Lillith, Serach, Bityah, and the Daughters of Z—teach us important values through their faith and actions.
9 x 12, 32 pp, Full-color illus., Hardcover, ISBN 1-879045-43-5 **$16.95** *For ages 8 & up*

Cain & Abel: Finding the Fruits of Peace
Full-color illus. by Joani Keller Rothenberg
Shows children that we have the power to deal with anger in positive ways. Provides questions for kids and adults to explore together.
9 x 12, 32 pp, Full-color illus., Hardcover, ISBN 1-58023-123-3 **$16.95** *For ages 5 & up*

God in Between
Full-color illus. by Sally Sweetland
If you wanted to find God, where would you look? This magical, mythical tale teaches that God can be found where we are: within all of us and the relationships between us.
9 x 12, 32 pp, Full-color illus., Hardcover, ISBN 1-879045-86-9 **$16.95** *For ages 4 & up*

God's Paintbrush
Wonderfully interactive, invites children of all faiths and backgrounds to encounter God through moments in their own lives. Provides questions adult and child can explore together.
11 x 8½, 32 pp, Full-color illus., Hardcover, ISBN 1-879045-22-2 **$16.95** *For ages 4 & up*

Also Available: **God's Paintbrush Teacher's Guide**
8½ x 11, 32 pp, PB, ISBN 1-879045-57-5 **$8.95**

God's Paintbrush Celebration Kit
A Spiritual Activity Kit for Teachers and Students of All Faiths, All Backgrounds
Additional activity sheets available:
8-Student Activity Sheet Pack (40 sheets/5 sessions), ISBN 1-58023-058-X **$19.95**
Single-Student Activity Sheet Pack (5 sessions), ISBN 1-58023-059-8 **$3.95**

In God's Name
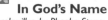
Full-color illus. by Phoebe Stone
Like an ancient myth in its poetic text and vibrant illustrations, this award-winning modern fable about the search for God's name celebrates the diversity and, at the same time, the unity of all people.
9 x 12, 32 pp, Full-color illus., Hardcover, ISBN 1-879045-26-5 **$16.95** *For ages 4 & up*

Also Available as a Board Book: **What Is God's Name?**
5 x 5, 24 pp, Board, Full-color illus., ISBN 1-893361-10-1 **$7.95** *For ages 0–4 (A SkyLight Paths book)*

Also Available: **In God's Name video and study guide**
Computer animation, original music, and children's voices. 18 min. **$29.99**

Also Available in Spanish: **El nombre de Dios**
9 x 12, 32 pp, Full-color illus., Hardcover, ISBN 1-893361-63-2 **$16.95** *(A SkyLight Paths book)*

Noah's Wife: The Story of Naamah
When God tells Noah to bring the animals of the world onto the ark, God also calls on Naamah, Noah's wife, to save each plant on Earth. Based on an ancient text.
9 x 12, 32 pp, Full-color illus., Hardcover, ISBN 1-58023-134-9 **$16.95** *For ages 4 & up*

Also Available as a Board Book: **Naamah, Noah's Wife**
5 x 5, 24 pp, Board, ISBN 1-893361-56-X **$7.95** *For ages 0–4 (A SkyLight Paths book)*

For Heaven's Sake: Finding God in Unexpected Places
9 x 12, 32 pp, Full-color illus., Hardcover, ISBN 1-58023-054-7 **$16.95** *For ages 4 & up*

God Said Amen: Finding the Answers to Our Prayers
9 x 12, 32 pp, Full-color illus., Hardcover, ISBN 1-58023-080-6 **$16.95** *For ages 4 & up*

Current Events/History

The Story of the Jews: A 4,000-Year Adventure—A Graphic History Book
Written & illustrated by Stan Mack
Through witty, illustrated narrative, we visit all the major happenings from biblical times to the twenty-first century. Celebrates the major characters and events that have shaped the Jewish people and culture.
6 x 9, 288 pp, illus., Quality PB, ISBN 1-58023-155-1 **$16.95**

The Jewish Prophet: Visionary Words from Moses and Miriam to Henrietta Szold and A. J. Heschel   *By Rabbi Michael J. Shire*   6½ x 8½, 128 pp, 123 full-color illus., Hardcover, ISBN 1-58023-168-3 **$25.00**

Shared Dreams: Martin Luther King, Jr. & the Jewish Community
By Rabbi Marc Schneier. Preface by Martin Luther King III.
6 x 9, 240 pp, Hardcover, ISBN 1-58023-062-8 **$24.95**

"Who Is a Jew?": Conversations, Not Conclusions   *By Meryl Hyman*
6 x 9, 272 pp, Quality PB, ISBN 1-58023-052-0 **$16.95**

Ecology

Ecology & the Jewish Spirit: Where Nature & the Sacred Meet
Edited by Ellen Bernstein   6 x 9, 288 pp, Quality PB, ISBN 1-58023-082-2 **$16.95**

Torah of the Earth: Exploring 4,000 Years of Ecology in Jewish Thought
Vol. 1: Biblical Israel: One Land, One People; Rabbinic Judaism: One People, Many Lands
Vol. 2: Zionism: One Land, Two Peoples; Eco-Judaism: One Earth, Many Peoples
Edited by Rabbi Arthur Waskow
Vol. 1: 6 x 9, 272 pp, Quality PB, ISBN 1-58023-086-5 **$19.95**
Vol. 2: 6 x 9, 336 pp, Quality PB, ISBN 1-58023-087-3 **$19.95**

Grief/Healing

Against the Dying of the Light: A Parent's Story of Love, Loss and Hope
By Leonard Fein
In this unusual exploration of heartbreak and healing, Leonard Fein chronicles the sudden death of his 30-year-old daughter and shares the hard-earned wisdom that emerges in the face of loss and grief.
5½ x 8½, 176 pp, Hardcover, ISBN 1-58023-110-1 **$19.95**

Grief in Our Seasons: A Mourner's Kaddish Companion   *By Rabbi Kerry M. Olitzky*
4½ x 6½, 448 pp, Quality PB, ISBN 1-879045-55-9 **$15.95**

Healing of Soul, Healing of Body: Spiritual Leaders Unfold the Strength & Solace in Psalms   *Edited by Rabbi Simkha Y. Weintraub, C.S.W.*
6 x 9, 128 pp, 2-color illus. text, Quality PB, ISBN 1-879045-31-1 **$14.95**

Jewish Paths toward Healing and Wholeness: A Personal Guide to Dealing with Suffering   *By Rabbi Kerry M. Olitzky. Foreword by Debbie Friedman.*
6 x 9, 192 pp, Quality PB, ISBN 1-58023-068-7 **$15.95**

Mourning & Mitzvah, 2nd Edition: A Guided Journal for Walking the Mourner's Path through Grief to Healing   *By Anne Brener, L.C.S.W.*
7½ x 9, 304 pp, Quality PB, ISBN 1-58023-113-6 **$19.95**

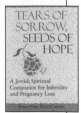

The Perfect Stranger's Guide to Funerals and Grieving Practices
A Guide to Etiquette in Other People's Religious Ceremonies   *Edited by Stuart M. Matlins*
6 x 9, 240 pp, Quality PB, ISBN 1-893361-20-9 **$16.95**   *(A SkyLight Paths book)*

Tears of Sorrow, Seeds of Hope: A Jewish Spiritual Companion for Infertility and Pregnancy Loss   *By Rabbi Nina Beth Cardin*
6 x 9, 192 pp, Hardcover, ISBN 1-58023-017-2 **$19.95**

A Time to Mourn, A Time to Comfort: A Guide to Jewish Bereavement and Comfort   *By Dr. Ron Wolfson*   7 x 9, 336 pp, Quality PB, ISBN 1-879045-96-6 **$18.95**

When a Grandparent Dies: A Kid's Own Remembering Workbook for Dealing with Shiva and the Year Beyond   *By Nechama Liss-Levinson, Ph.D.*
8 x 10, 48 pp, 2-color text, Hardcover, ISBN 1-879045-44-3 **$15.95**   *For ages 7–13*

Abraham Joshua Heschel

The Earth Is the Lord's: The Inner World of the Jew in Eastern Europe
5½ x 8, 128 pp, Quality PB, ISBN 1-879045-42-7 **$14.95**

Israel: An Echo of Eternity New Introduction by Susannah Heschel
5½ x 8, 272 pp, Quality PB, ISBN 1-879045-70-2 **$19.95**

A Passion for Truth: Despair and Hope in Hasidism
5½ x 8, 352 pp, Quality PB, ISBN 1-879045-41-9 **$18.95**

Holidays/Holy Days

7th Heaven: Celebrating Shabbat with Rebbe Nachman of Breslov
By Moshe Mykoff with the Breslov Research Institute
Based on the teachings of Rebbe Nachman of Breslov. Explores the art of consciously observing Shabbat and understanding in-depth many of the day's traditional spiritual practices.
5⅛ x 8¼, 224 pp, Deluxe PB w/flaps, ISBN 1-58023-175-6 **$18.95**

The Women's Passover Companion
Women's Reflections on the Festival of Freedom
Edited by Rabbi Sharon Cohen Anisfeld, Tara Mohr, and Catherine Spector
A groundbreaking collection that captures the voices of Jewish women who engage in a provocative conversation about women's relationships to Passover as well as the roots and meanings of women's seders.
6 x 9, 352 pp, Hardcover, ISBN 1-58023-128-4 **$24.95**

The Women's Seder Sourcebook
Rituals & Readings for Use at the Passover Seder
Edited by Rabbi Sharon Cohen Anisfeld, Tara Mohr, and Catherine Spector
This practical guide gathers the voices of more than one hundred women in readings, personal and creative reflections, commentaries, blessings, and ritual suggestions that can be incorporated into your Passover celebration as supplements to or substitutes for traditional passages of the haggadah.
6 x 9, 384 pp, Hardcover, ISBN 1-58023-136-5 **$24.95**

Hanukkah, 2nd Edition: The Family Guide to Spiritual Celebration
By Dr. Ron Wolfson. Edited by Joel Lurie Grishaver.
7 x 9, 240 pp, illus., Quality PB, ISBN 1-58023-122-5 **$18.95**

The Jewish Gardening Cookbook: Growing Plants & Cooking for
Holidays & Festivals *By Michael Brown*
6 x 9, 224 pp, 30+ illus., Quality PB, ISBN 1-58023-116-0 **$16.95;**
Hardcover, ISBN 1-58023-004-0 **$21.95**

Passover, 2nd Edition: The Family Guide to Spiritual Celebration
By Dr. Ron Wolfson with Joel Lurie Grishaver
7 x 9, 352 pp, Quality PB, ISBN 1-58023-174-8 **$19.95**

Shabbat, 2nd Edition: The Family Guide to Preparing for and Celebrating the Sabbath
By Dr. Ron Wolfson 7 x 9, 320 pp, illus., Quality PB, ISBN 1-58023-164-0 **$19.95**

Sharing Blessings: Children's Stories for Exploring the Spirit of the Jewish Holidays
By Rahel Musleah and Michael Klayman
8½ x 11, 64 pp, Full-color illus., Hardcover, ISBN 1-879045-71-0 **$18.95** *For ages 6 & up*

The Jewish Family Fun Book: Holiday Projects, Everyday Activities,
and Travel Ideas with Jewish Themes

By Danielle Dardashti and Roni Sarig. Illus. by Avi Katz.
With almost 100 easy-to-do activities to re-invigorate age-old Jewish customs and make them fun for the whole family, this complete sourcebook details activities for fun at home and away from home, including meaningful everyday and holiday crafts, recipes, travel guides, enriching entertainment and much, much more. Illustrated.
6 x 9, 288 pp, 70+ b/w illus. & diagrams, Quality PB, ISBN 1-58023-171-3 **$18.95**

Inspiration

God in All Moments
Mystical & Practical Spiritual Wisdom from Hasidic Masters
Edited and translated by Or N. Rose with Ebn D. Leader
Hasidic teachings on how to be mindful in religious practice and how to cultivate everyday ethical behavior—*hanhagot.*
5½ x 8½, 192 pp, Quality PB, ISBN 1-58023-186-1 **$16.95**

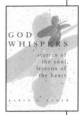

The Dance of the Dolphin: Finding Prayer, Perspective and Meaning in the Stories of Our Lives *By Karyn D. Kedar* 6 x 9, 176 pp, Hardcover, ISBN 1-58023-154-3 **$19.95**

The Empty Chair: Finding Hope and Joy—Timeless Wisdom from a Hasidic Master, Rebbe Nachman of Breslov *Adapted by Moshe Mykoff and the Breslov Research Institute*
4 x 6, 128 pp, 2-color text, Deluxe PB w/flaps, ISBN 1-879045-67-2 **$9.95**

The Gentle Weapon: Prayers for Everyday and Not-So-Everyday Moments— Timeless Wisdom from the Teachings of the Hasidic Master, Rebbe Nachman of Breslov
Adapted by Moshe Mykoff and S. C. Mizrahi, together with the Breslov Research Institute
4 x 6, 144 pp, 2-color text, Deluxe PB w/flaps, ISBN 1-58023-022-9 **$9.95**

God Whispers: Stories of the Soul, Lessons of the Heart *By Karyn D. Kedar*
6 x 9, 176 pp, Quality PB, ISBN 1-58023-088-1 **$15.95**

An Orphan in History: One Man's Triumphant Search for His Jewish Roots
By Paul Cowan. Afterword by Rachel Cowan. 6 x 9, 288 pp, Quality PB, ISBN 1-58023-135-7 **$16.95**

Restful Reflections: Nighttime Inspiration to Calm the Soul, Based on Jewish Wisdom
By Rabbi Kerry M. Olitzky & Rabbi Lori Forman
4½ x 6½, 448 pp, Quality PB, ISBN 1-58023-091-1 **$15.95**

Sacred Intentions: Daily Inspiration to Strengthen the Spirit, Based on Jewish Wisdom
By Rabbi Kerry M. Olitzky and Rabbi Lori Forman
4½ x 6½, 448 pp, Quality PB, ISBN 1-58023-061-X **$15.95**

Kabbalah/Mysticism/Enneagram

Seek My Face: A Jewish Mystical Theology
By Dr. Arthur Green
This classic work of contemporary Jewish theology, revised and updated, is a profound, deeply personal statement of the lasting truths of Jewish mysticism and the basic faith claims of Judaism. A tool for anyone seeking the elusive presence of God in the world. 6 x 9, 304 pp, Quality PB, ISBN 1-58023-130-6 **$19.95**

Zohar: Annotated & Explained
Translation and annotation by Dr. Daniel C. Matt. Foreword by Andrew Harvey, SkyLight Illuminations series editor.
Offers insightful yet unobtrusive commentary to the masterpiece of Jewish mysticism that explains references and mystical symbols, shares wisdom of spiritual masters, and clarifies the *Zohar*'s bold claim: We have always been taught that we need God, but in order to manifest in the world, God needs us.
5½ x 8½, 160 pp, Quality PB, ISBN 1-893361-51-9 **$15.95** *(A SkyLight Paths book)*

Cast in God's Image: Discover Your Personality Type Using the Enneagram and Kabbalah
By Rabbi Howard A. Addison
7 x 9, 176 pp, Quality PB, Layflat binding, 20+ journaling exercises, ISBN 1-58023-124-1 **$16.95**

Ehyeh: A Kabbalah for Tomorrow *By Dr. Arthur Green*
6 x 9, 224 pp, Hardcover, ISBN 1-58023-125-X **$21.95**

The Enneagram and Kabbalah: Reading Your Soul *By Rabbi Howard A. Addison*
6 x 9, 176 pp, Quality PB, ISBN 1-58023-001-6 **$15.95**

Finding Joy: A Practical Spiritual Guide to Happiness *By Dannel I. Schwartz with Mark Hass*
6 x 9, 192 pp, Quality PB, ISBN 1-58023-009-1 **$14.95**; Hardcover, ISBN 1-879045-53-2 **$19.95**

The Gift of Kabbalah: Discovering the Secrets of Heaven, Renewing Your Life on Earth
By Tamar Frankiel, Ph.D.
6 x 9, 256 pp, Quality PB, ISBN 1-58023-141-1 **$16.95**; Hardcover, ISBN 1-58023-108-X **$21.95**

The Way Into Jewish Mystical Tradition *By Lawrence Kushner*
6 x 9, 224 pp, Hardcover, ISBN 1-58023-029-6 **$21.95**

Life Cycle

Parenting

The New Jewish Baby Album: Creating and Celebrating the Beginning of a Spiritual Life—A Jewish Lights Companion
By the Editors at Jewish Lights. Foreword by Anita Diamant. Preface by Sandy Eisenberg Sasso.
A spiritual keepsake that will be treasured for generations. More than just a memory book, *shows you how—and why it's important*—to create a Jewish home and a Jewish life. Includes sections to describe naming ceremony, space to write encouragements, and pages for writing original blessings, prayers, and meaningful quotes throughout.
8 x 10, 64 pp, Deluxe Padded Hardcover, Full-color illus., ISBN 1-58023-138-1 **$19.95**

The Jewish Pregnancy Book: A Resource for the Soul, Body & Mind during Pregnancy, Birth & the First Three Months
By Sandy Falk, M.D., and Rabbi Daniel Judson, with Steven A. Rapp
Includes medical information on fetal development, pre-natal testing and more, from a liberal Jewish perspective; prenatal *Aleph-Bet* yoga; and ancient and modern prayers and rituals for each stage of pregnancy.
7 x 10, 208 pp, Quality PB, b/w illus., ISBN 1-58023-178-0 **$16.95**

Celebrating Your New Jewish Daughter: Creating Jewish Ways to Welcome Baby Girls into the Covenant—New and Traditional Ceremonies
By Debra Nussbaum Cohen 6 x 9, 272 pp, Quality PB, ISBN 1-58023-090-3 **$18.95**

The New Jewish Baby Book: Names, Ceremonies & Customs—A Guide for Today's Families By Anita Diamant 6 x 9, 336 pp, Quality PB, ISBN 1-879045-28-1 **$18.95**

Parenting As a Spiritual Journey: Deepening Ordinary and Extraordinary Events into Sacred Occasions By Rabbi Nancy Fuchs-Kreimer
6 x 9, 224 pp, Quality PB, ISBN 1-58023-016-4 **$16.95**

Embracing the Covenant: Converts to Judaism Talk About Why & How
Edited and with introductions by Rabbi Allan Berkowitz and Patti Moskovitz
6 x 9, 192 pp, Quality PB, ISBN 1-879045-50-8 **$16.95**

The Guide to Jewish Interfaith Family Life: An InterfaithFamily.com Handbook
Edited by Ronnie Friedland and Edmund Case 6 x 9, 384 pp, Quality PB, ISBN 1-58023-153-5 **$18.95**

Making a Successful Jewish Interfaith Marriage: The Jewish Outreach Institute Guide to Opportunities, Challenges and Resources
By Rabbi Kerry Olitzky with Joan Peterson Littman 6 x 9, 176 pp, Quality PB, ISBN 1-58023-170-5 **$16.95**

The Perfect Stranger's Guide to Wedding Ceremonies
A Guide to Etiquette in Other People's Religious Ceremonies Edited by Stuart M. Matlins
6 x 9, 208 pp, Quality PB, ISBN 1-893361-19-5 **$16.95** (A SkyLight Paths book)

How to Be a Perfect Stranger, 3rd Edition
The Essential Religious Etiquette Handbook
Edited by Stuart M. Matlins and Arthur J. Magida
The indispensable guidebook to help the well-meaning guest when visiting other people's religious ceremonies.
A straightforward guide to the rituals and celebrations of the major religions and denominations in the United States and Canada from the perspective of an interested guest of any other faith, based on information obtained from authorities of each religion. Belongs in every living room, library, and office.
6 x 9, 432 pp, Quality PB, ISBN 1-893361-67-5 **$19.95** (A SkyLight Paths book)

Divorce Is a Mitzvah: A Practical Guide to Finding Wholeness and Holiness When Your Marriage Dies By Rabbi Perry Netter. Afterword by Rabbi Laura Geller.
6 x 9, 224 pp, Quality PB, ISBN 1-58023-172-1 **$16.95**

A Heart of Wisdom: Making the Jewish Journey from Midlife through the Elder Years
Edited by Susan Berrin. Foreword by Harold Kushner. 6 x 9, 384 pp, Quality PB, ISBN 1-58023-051-2 **$18.95**

So That Your Values Live On: Ethical Wills and How to Prepare Them
Edited by Jack Riemer and Nathaniel Stampfer 6 x 9, 272 pp, Quality PB, ISBN 1-879045-34-6 **$18.95**

Meditation

The Handbook of Jewish Meditation Practices
A Guide for Enriching the Sabbath and Other Days of Your Life
By Rabbi David A. Cooper
Easy-to-learn meditation techniques for use on the Sabbath and every day, to help us return to the roots of traditional Jewish spirituality where Shabbat is a state of mind and soul.   6 x 9, 208 pp, Quality PB, ISBN 1-58023-102-0 **$16.95**

Discovering Jewish Meditation: Instruction & Guidance for Learning an Ancient Spiritual Practice *By Nan Fink Gefen, Ph.D.* 6 x 9, 208 pp, Quality PB, ISBN 1-58023-067-9 **$16.95**

A Heart of Stillness: A Complete Guide to Learning the Art of Meditation
By Rabbi David A. Cooper
5½ x 8½, 272 pp, Quality PB, ISBN 1-893361-03-9 **$16.95**   *(A SkyLight Paths book)*

Meditation from the Heart of Judaism: Today's Teachers Share Their
Practices, Techniques, and Faith   *Edited by Avram Davis*
6 x 9, 256 pp, Quality PB, ISBN 1-58023-049-0 **$16.95**

Silence, Simplicity & Solitude: A Complete Guide to Spiritual Retreat at Home
By Rabbi David A. Cooper
5½ x 8½, 336 pp, Quality PB, ISBN 1-893361-04-7 **$16.95**   *(A SkyLight Paths book)*

Three Gates to Meditation Practice: A Personal Journey into Sufism,
Buddhism, and Judaism   *By Rabbi David A. Cooper*
5½ x 8½, 240 pp, Quality PB, ISBN 1-893361-22-5 **$16.95**   *(A SkyLight Paths book)*

The Way of Flame: A Guide to the Forgotten Mystical Tradition of Jewish Meditation
By Avram Davis 4½ x 8, 176 pp, Quality PB, ISBN 1-58023-060-1 **$15.95**

Ritual/Sacred Practice

The Jewish Dream Book
The Key to Opening the Inner Meaning of Your Dreams
By Vanessa L. Ochs with Elizabeth Ochs; Full-color Illus. by Kristina Swarner
Vibrant illustrations, instructions for how modern people can perform ancient Jewish dream practices, and dream interpretations drawn from the Jewish wisdom tradition help make this guide the ideal bedside companion for anyone who wants to further their understanding of their dreams—and themselves.
8 x 8, 120 pp, Full-color illus., Deluxe PB w/flaps, ISBN 1-58023-132-2 **$16.95**

The Rituals & Practices of a Jewish Life: A Handbook for Personal Spiritual
Renewal   *Edited by Rabbi Kerry M. Olitzky and Rabbi Daniel Judson*
6 x 9, 272 pp, illus., Quality PB, ISBN 1-58023-169-1 **$18.95**

The Book of Jewish Sacred Practices: CLAL's Guide to Everyday & Holiday
Rituals & Blessings   *Edited by Rabbi Irwin Kula and Vanessa L. Ochs, Ph.D.*
6 x 9, 368 pp, Quality PB, ISBN 1-58023-152-7 **$18.95**

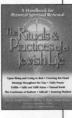

Science Fiction/
Mystery & Detective Fiction

Mystery Midrash: An Anthology of Jewish Mystery & Detective Fiction
Edited by Lawrence W. Raphael. Preface by Joel Siegel.
6 x 9, 304 pp, Quality PB, ISBN 1-58023-055-5 **$16.95**

Criminal Kabbalah: An Intriguing Anthology of Jewish Mystery & Detective Fiction
Edited by Lawrence W. Raphael. Foreword by Laurie R. King.
6 x 9, 256 pp, Quality PB, ISBN 1-58023-109-8 **$16.95**

More Wandering Stars: An Anthology of Outstanding Stories of Jewish Fantasy and
Science Fiction   *Edited by Jack Dann. Introduction by Isaac Asimov.*
6 x 9, 192 pp, Quality PB, ISBN 1-58023-063-6 **$16.95**

Wandering Stars: An Anthology of Jewish Fantasy & Science Fiction
Edited by Jack Dann. Introduction by Isaac Asimov.
6 x 9, 272 pp, Quality PB, ISBN 1-58023-005-9 **$16.95**

Spirituality

The Alphabet of Paradise: An A–Z of Spirituality for Everyday Life
By Rabbi Howard Cooper

In twenty-six engaging chapters, Cooper spiritually illuminates the subjects of our daily lives—A to Z—examining these sources by using an ancient Jewish mystical method of interpretation that reveals both the literal and more allusive meanings of each.   5 x 7¼, 224 pp, Quality PB, ISBN 1-893361-80-2 **$16.95** *(A SkyLight Paths book)*

Does the Soul Survive?: A Jewish Journey to Belief in Afterlife, Past Lives & Living with Purpose   By Rabbi Elie Kaplan Spitz. Foreword by Brian L Weiss, M.D.

Spitz relates his own experiences and those shared with him by people he has worked with as a rabbi, and shows us that belief in afterlife and past lives, so often approached with reluctance, is in fact true to Jewish tradition.
6 x 9, 288 pp, Quality PB, ISBN 1-58023-165-9 **$16.95**; Hardcover, ISBN 1-58023-094-6 **$21.95**

First Steps to a New Jewish Spirit: Reb Zalman's Guide to Recapturing the Intimacy & Ecstasy in Your Relationship with God
By Rabbi Zalman M. Schachter-Shalomi with Donald Gropman

An extraordinary spiritual handbook that restores psychic and physical vigor by introducing us to new models and alternative ways of practicing Judaism. Offers meditation and contemplation exercises for enriching the most important aspects of everyday life.   6 x 9, 144 pp, Quality PB, ISBN 1-58023-182-9 **$16.95**

God in Our Relationships: Spirituality between People from the Teachings of Martin Buber   By Rabbi Dennis S. Ross

On the eightieth anniversary of Buber's classic work, we can discover new answers to critical issues in our lives. Inspiring examples from Ross's own life—as congregational rabbi, father, hospital chaplain, social worker, and husband—illustrate Buber's difficult-to-understand ideas about how we encounter God and each other. 5½ x 8½, 160 pp, Quality PB, ISBN 1-58023-147-0 **$16.95**

The Jewish Lights Spirituality Handbook: A Guide to Understanding, Exploring & Living a Spiritual Life   Edited by Stuart M. Matlins

What exactly is "Jewish" about spirituality? How do I make it a part of my life? Fifty of today's foremost spiritual leaders share their ideas and experience with us.
6 x 9, 456 pp, Quality PB, ISBN 1-58023-093-8 **$19.95**; Hardcover, ISBN 1-58023-100-4 **$24.95**

Bringing the Psalms to Life: How to Understand and Use the Book of Psalms
By Dr. Daniel F. Polish
6 x 9, 208 pp, Quality PB, ISBN 1-58023-157-8 **$16.95**; Hardcover, ISBN 1-58023-077-6 **$21.95**

God & the Big Bang: Discovering Harmony between Science & Spirituality
By Dr. Daniel C. Matt   6 x 9, 216 pp, Quality PB, ISBN 1-879045-89-3 **$16.95**

Godwrestling—Round 2: Ancient Wisdom, Future Paths
By Rabbi Arthur Waskow   6 x 9, 352 pp, Quality PB, ISBN 1-879045-72-9 **$18.95**

One God Clapping: The Spiritual Path of a Zen Rabbi   By Rabbi Alan Lew with Sherril Jaffe
5½ x 8½, 336 pp, Quality PB, ISBN 1-58023-115-2 **$16.95**

The Path of Blessing: Experiencing the Energy and Abundance of the Divine
By Rabbi Marcia Prager   5½ x 8½, 240 pp., Quality PB, ISBN 1-58023-148-9 **$16.95**

Six Jewish Spiritual Paths: A Rationalist Looks at Spirituality   By Rabbi Rifat Sonsino
6 x 9, 208 pp, Quality PB, ISBN 1-58023-167-5 **$16.95**; Hardcover, ISBN 1-58023-095-4 **$21.95**

Soul Judaism: Dancing with God into a New Era
By Rabbi Wayne Dosick   5½ x 8½, 304 pp, Quality PB, ISBN 1-58023-053-9 **$16.95**

Stepping Stones to Jewish Spiritual Living: Walking the Path Morning, Noon, and Night   By Rabbi James L. Mirel and Karen Bonnell Werth
6 x 9, 240 pp, Quality PB, ISBN 1-58023-074-1 **$16.95**; Hardcover, ISBN 1-58023-003-2 **$21.95**

There Is No Messiah... and You're It: The Stunning Transformation of Judaism's Most Provocative Idea   By Rabbi Robert N. Levine, D.D.
6 x 9, 192 pp, Hardcover, ISBN 1-58023-173-X **$21.95**

These Are the Words: A Vocabulary of Jewish Spiritual Life   By Dr. Arthur Green
6 x 9, 304 pp, Quality PB, ISBN 1-58023-107-1 **$18.95**

Spirituality/Lawrence Kushner

The Book of Letters: A Mystical Hebrew Alphabet
Popular Hardcover Edition, 6 x 9, 80 pp, 2-color text, ISBN 1-879045-00-1 **$24.95**
Deluxe Gift Edition with slipcase, 9 x 12, 80 pp, 4-color text, Hardcover, ISBN 1-879045-01-X **$79.95**
Collector's Limited Edition, 9 x 12, 80 pp, gold foil embossed pages, w/limited edition silkscreened
print, ISBN 1-879045-04-4 **$349.00**

The Book of Miracles: A Young Person's Guide to Jewish Spiritual Awareness
All-new illustrations by the author
6 x 9, 96 pp, 2-color illus., Hardcover, ISBN 1-879045-78-8 **$16.95** *For ages 9–13*

The Book of Words: Talking Spiritual Life, Living Spiritual Talk
6 x 9, 160 pp, Quality PB, ISBN 1-58023-020-2 **$16.95**

Eyes Remade for Wonder: A Lawrence Kushner Reader
Introduction by Thomas Moore
6 x 9, 240 pp, Quality PB, ISBN 1-58023-042-3 **$18.95**; Hardcover, ISBN 1-58023-014-8 **$23.95**

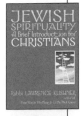

God Was in This Place & I, i Did Not Know
Finding Self, Spirituality and Ultimate Meaning
6 x 9, 192 pp, Quality PB, ISBN 1-879045-33-8 **$16.95**

Honey from the Rock: An Introduction to Jewish Mysticism
6 x 9, 176 pp, Quality PB, ISBN 1-58023-073-3 **$16.95**

Invisible Lines of Connection: Sacred Stories of the Ordinary
5½ x 8½, 160 pp, Quality PB, ISBN 1-879045-98-2 **$15.95**

Jewish Spirituality—A Brief Introduction for Christians
5½ x 8½, 112 pp, Quality PB Original, ISBN 1-58023-150-0 **$12.95**

The River of Light: Jewish Mystical Awareness
6 x 9, 192 pp, Quality PB, ISBN 1-58023-096-2 **$16.95**

The Way Into Jewish Mystical Tradition
6 x 9, 224 pp, Hardcover, ISBN 1-58023-029-6 **$21.95**

Spirituality/Prayer

Pray Tell: A Hadassah Guide to Jewish Prayer
*By Rabbi Jules Harlow, with contributions from Tamara Cohen, Rochelle Furstenberg, Rabbi Daniel
Gordis, Leora Tanenbaum, and many others*
A guide to traditional Jewish prayer enriched with insight and wisdom from a
broad variety of viewpoints—from Orthodox, Conservative, Reform, and
Reconstructionist Judaism to New Age and feminist. Offers fresh and modern
slants on what it means to pray as a Jew, and how women and men might actu-
ally pray.   8½ x 11, 400 pp, Quality PB, ISBN 1-58023-163-2 **$29.95**

My People's Prayer Book Series
Traditional Prayers, Modern Commentaries
Edited by Rabbi Lawrence A. Hoffman
Provides diverse and exciting commentary to the traditional liturgy, helping modern
men and women find new wisdom in Jewish prayer, and bring liturgy into their lives.
Each book includes Hebrew text, modern translation, and
commentaries from all perspectives of the Jewish world.

Vol. 1—The *Sh'ma* and Its Blessings
   7 x 10, 168 pp, Hardcover, ISBN 1-879045-79-6 **$23.95**
Vol. 2—The *Amidah*
   7 x 10, 240 pp, Hardcover, ISBN 1-879045-80-X **$24.95**
Vol. 3—*P'sukei D'zimrah* (Morning Psalms)
   7 x 10, 240 pp, Hardcover, ISBN 1-879045-81-8 **$24.95**
Vol. 4—*Seder K'riat Hatorah* (The Torah Service)
   7 x 10, 264 pp, Hardcover, ISBN 1-879045-82-6 **$23.95**
Vol. 5—*Birkhot Hashachar* (Morning Blessings)
   7 x 10, 240 pp, Hardcover, ISBN 1-879045-83-4 **$24.95**
Vol. 6—*Tachanun* and Concluding Prayers
   7 x 10, 240 pp, Hardcover, ISBN 1-879045-84-2 **$24.95**
Vol. 7—Shabbat at Home
   7 x 10, 240 pp, Hardcover, ISBN 1-879045-85-0 **$24.95**

Spirituality/The Way Into... Series

The Way Into... Series offers an accessible and highly usable "guided tour" of the Jewish faith, people, history and beliefs—in total, an introduction to Judaism that will enable you to understand and interact with the sacred texts of the Jewish tradition. Each volume is written by a leading contemporary scholar and teacher, and explores one key aspect of Judaism. The Way Into... enables all readers to achieve a real sense of Jewish cultural literacy through guided study.

The Way Into Encountering God in Judaism By Neil Gillman
6 x 9, 240 pp, Hardcover, ISBN 1-58023-025-3 **$21.95**

Also Available: **The Jewish Approach to God: A Brief Introduction for Christians**
By Neil Gillman 5½ x 8¼, 192 pp, Quality PB, ISBN 1-58023-190-X **$16.95**

The Way Into Jewish Mystical Tradition By Lawrence Kushner
6 x 9, 224 pp, Hardcover, ISBN 1-58023-029-6 **$21.95**

The Way Into Jewish Prayer By Lawrence A. Hoffman
6 x 9, 224 pp, Hardcover, ISBN 1-58023-027-X **$21.95**

The Way Into Torah By Norman J. Cohen
6 x 9, 176 pp, Hardcover, ISBN 1-58023-028-8 **$21.95**

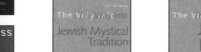  

Spirituality in the Workplace

Being God's Partner
How to Find the Hidden Link Between Spirituality and Your Work
By Rabbi Jeffrey K. Salkin. Introduction by Norman Lear.
6 x 9, 192 pp, Quality PB, ISBN 1-879045-65-6 **$17.95**

The Business Bible: 10 New Commandments for Bringing Spirituality & Ethical Values into the Workplace By Rabbi Wayne Dosick
5½ x 8¼, 208 pp, Quality PB, ISBN 1-58023-101-2 **$14.95**

Spirituality and Wellness

Aleph-Bet Yoga
Embodying the Hebrew Letters for Physical and Spiritual Well-Being
By Steven A. Rapp. Foreword by Tamar Frankiel, Ph.D., and Judy Greenfeld. Preface by Hart Lazer
7 x 10, 128 pp, b/w photos, Quality PB, Layflat binding, ISBN 1-58023-162-4 **$16.95**

Entering the Temple of Dreams
Jewish Prayers, Movements, and Meditations for the End of the Day
By Tamar Frankiel, Ph.D., and Judy Greenfeld
7 x 10, 192 pp, illus., Quality PB, ISBN 1-58023-079-2 **$16.95**

Minding the Temple of the Soul
Balancing Body, Mind, and Spirit through Traditional Jewish Prayer, Movement, and Meditation By Tamar Frankiel, Ph.D., and Judy Greenfeld
7 x 10, 184 pp, illus., Quality PB, ISBN 1-879045-64-8 **$16.95**
Audiotape of the Blessings and Meditations: 60 min. **$9.95**
Videotape of the Movements and Meditations: 46 min. **$20.00**

Spirituality/Women's Interest

Lifecycles, Vol. 1: Jewish Women on Life Passages & Personal Milestones
Edited and with introductions by Rabbi Debra Orenstein
6 x 9, 480 pp, Quality PB, ISBN 1-58023-018-0 **$19.95**

Lifecycles, Vol. 2: Jewish Women on Biblical Themes in Contemporary Life
Edited and with introductions by Rabbi Debra Orenstein and Rabbi Jane Rachel Litman
6 x 9, 464 pp, Quality PB, ISBN 1-58023-019-9 **$19.95**

Moonbeams: A Hadassah Rosh Hodesh Guide   *Edited by Carol Diament, Ph.D.*
8½ x 11, 240 pp, Quality PB, ISBN 1-58023-099-7 **$20.00**

ReVisions: Seeing Torah through a Feminist Lens   *By Rabbi Elyse Goldstein*
5½ x 8½, 224 pp, Quality PB, ISBN 1-58023-117-9 **$16.95**

White Fire: A Portrait of Women Spiritual Leaders in America
By Rabbi Malka Drucker. Photographs by Gay Block.
7 x 10, 320 pp, 30+ b/w photos, Hardcover, ISBN 1-893361-64-0 **$24.95** *(A SkyLight Paths book)*

Women of the Wall: Claiming Sacred Ground at Judaism's Holy Site
Edited by Phyllis Chesler and Rivka Haut
6 x 9, 496 pp, b/w photos, Hardcover, ISBN 1-58023-161-6 **$34.95**

The Women's Torah Commentary: New Insights from Women Rabbis on the 54
Weekly Torah Portions   *Edited by Rabbi Elyse Goldstein*
6 x 9, 496 pp, Hardcover, ISBN 1-58023-076-8 **$34.95**

The Year Mom Got Religion: One Woman's Midlife Journey into Judaism
By Lee Meyerhoff Hendler
6 x 9, 208 pp, Quality PB, ISBN 1-58023-070-9 **$15.95**; Hardcover, ISBN 1-58023-000-8 **$19.95**

See Holidays for *The Women's Passover Companion: Women's Reflections on the Festival of Freedom* and *The Women's Seder Sourcebook: Rituals & Readings for Use at the Passover Seder.*

Theology/Philosophy

Aspects of Rabbinic Theology
By Solomon Schechter. New Introduction by Dr. Neil Gillman.
6 x 9, 448 pp, Quality PB, ISBN 1-879045-24-9 **$19.95**

Broken Tablets: Restoring the Ten Commandments and Ourselves
Edited by Rachel S. Mikva. Introduction by Lawrence Kushner. Afterword by Arnold Jacob Wolf.
6 x 9, 192 pp, Quality PB, ISBN 1-58023-158-6 **$16.95**; Hardcover, ISBN 1-58023-066-0 **$21.95**

Creating an Ethical Jewish Life
A Practical Introduction to Classic Teachings on How to Be a Jew
By Dr. Byron L. Sherwin and Seymour J. Cohen
6 x 9, 336 pp, Quality PB, ISBN 1-58023-114-4 **$19.95**

The Death of Death: Resurrection and Immortality in Jewish Thought
By Dr. Neil Gillman   6 x 9, 336 pp, Quality PB, ISBN 1-58023-081-4 **$18.95**

Evolving Halakhah: A Progressive Approach to Traditional Jewish Law
By Rabbi Dr. Moshe Zemer
6 x 9, 480 pp, Quality PB, ISBN 1-58023-127-6 **$29.95**; Hardcover, ISBN 1-58023-002-4 **$40.00**

Hasidic Tales: Annotated & Explained
By Rabbi Rami Shapiro. Foreword by Andrew Harvey, SkyLight Illuminations series editor.
5½ x 8½, 192 pp, Quality PB, ISBN 1-893361-86-1 **$16.95** *(A SkyLight Paths Book)*

A Heart of Many Rooms: Celebrating the Many Voices within Judaism
By Dr. David Hartman
6 x 9, 352 pp, Quality PB, ISBN 1-58023-156-X **$19.95**; Hardcover, ISBN 1-58023-048-2 **$24.95**

Judaism and Modern Man: An Interpretation of Jewish Religion
By Will Herberg. New Introduction by Dr. Neil Gillman.
5½ x 8½, 336 pp, Quality PB, ISBN 1-879045-87-7 **$18.95**

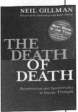

Keeping Faith with the Psalms: Deepen Your Relationship with God Using the
Book of Psalms   *By Daniel F. Polish*
6 x 9, 272 pp, Hardcover, ISBN 1-58023-179-9 **$24.95**

About Jewish Lights

People of all faiths and backgrounds yearn for books that attract, engage, educate, and spiritually inspire.

Our principal goal is to stimulate thought and help all people learn about who the Jewish People are, where they come from, and what the future can be made to hold   rimary audience, our b   ill broaden their under

We   ual thought and experi   say it in a voice that y

Our   , stimulate, and inspire   ks are beautiful and c   a difference in your l

For   k we have provided   ing and useful. They

ractice

ophy

ins, Publisher

blishing
nt 05091
.com
day–Friday)

m